PRACTICAL EM
FOR COLLABORATION AND C

Indi Young

Rosenfeld Media
Brooklyn, New York

Practical Empathy

For Collaboration and Creativity in Your Work

By Indi Young

Rosenfeld Media, LLC

457 Third Street, #4R

Brooklyn, New York

11215 USA

On the Web: www.rosenfeldmedia.com

Please send errors to: errata@rosenfeldmedia.com

Publisher: Louis Rosenfeld

Managing Editor: Marta Justak

Interior Layout Tech: Danielle Foster

Cover Design: The Heads of State

Indexer: Sharon Shock

Proofreader: Sue Boshers

Illustrations: Brad Colbow

ISBN: 1-933820-48-9

ISBN-13: 978-1-933820-48-4

LCCN: 2014955523

Printed and bound in the United States of America

For all the engineers, designers, writers, craftspeople, problem-solvers, managers, organizers, and leaders who have the honesty and passion to help others, to make stuff happen, and to make it work better. Your energy and enthusiasm sustains everyone around you.

Also to Matt Stephens
August 10, 1964–March 30, 2010

HOW TO USE THIS BOOK

Who Should Read This Book?

This book is for developers, designers, writers, and decision-makers. It's a book about developing and applying empathy *in your work*, which means there is a broad range of things you can use it for. It can help you improve the things you make: policies, processes, products, services, and written content. It can help you improve the way you interact with people. So if you are involved in any of these things at work (and who isn't?), this book is meant for you. Additionally, the phrase *in your work* can represent the things you do that you don't necessarily get paid for: volunteer work, class projects, hobbies, clubs, associations, etc. So the empathy skills you learn in this book will bleed into areas of your life far beyond what is traditionally considered to be a paid career.

This book will help you become more aware of your unconscious habits. If you are in a frame of mind where you're able to make some internal changes to your own thinking, this book is for you. It will help you become more mentally and emotionally mature. If you're not in that frame of mind, the concepts in this book will provide you with a solid framework for improving your career skills.

If you are a manager of any type—responsible for a group of people or accountable for certain numbers on your organization's profit-and-loss report—this book is for you. It will help you support the people on your team in a way that will help them shine. And it will help you see a path forward through the jungle of options that will more faithfully and successfully support the people you are trying to help.

What's in This Book?

There are nine chapters in this book grouped into three areas:

- What role does empathy play in your work?
- Developing empathy
- Applying empathy (in the things you create, as you collaborate, and within your organization as a whole)

What Role Does Empathy Play in Your Work?

Chapter 1, "Business Is Out of Balance," outlines the core reasons why focusing only on numeric measurements and scientific-sounding reassurances blinds your decision-making and communication clarity. Including word-based explanations paints the "why" half of the picture.

Chapter 2, "Empathy Brings Balance," explains how empathy is not just walking in someone's shoes. You must first develop empathy to be able to wield it.

Chapter 3, "Put Empathy to Work," demonstrates how empathy feeds into your development cycles. You can develop and apply empathy purely within your mind, or you can develop written artifacts that will remind you or your team of what you learned.

Developing Empathy

Chapter 4, "A New Way to Listen," contains guidelines for your practice of listening. A good listener concentrates only on what is being said, and this support establishes trust and rapport.

Chapter 5, "Make Sense of What You Heard," makes the case for reviewing each story and writing summaries of the concepts, as a way of letting your understanding of each person simmer and deepen. Summarizing is an optional, but powerful, way to clarify your understanding and also see where you can improve your listening skills.

Applying Empathy

Chapter 6, "Apply Empathy to What You Create," covers how to find patterns in your listening sessions and then use those patterns to clarify behavioral audience segments and inspire ideas. An empathetic mindset helps you encourage others to solve more varied, enduring challenges.

Chapter 7, "Apply Empathy with People at Work," encourages you to employ listening sessions to better understand and support your peers, your direct reports, and your higher-ups. Awareness of your own reactions and the reactions of other people will help you improve your collaboration style.

Chapter 8, "Apply Empathy Within Your Organization," walks you through a series of paths you might take within your organization to make small changes and blaze a trail away from the competition. Moving past a focus on technology and methods will help your organization think its own thoughts about the problems that could be solved.

Chapter 9, "Where Do You Go from Here?" emphasizes "going small" and slowly mixing the empathetic mindset into your normal work.

What Comes with This Book?

This book's companion website (rosenfeldmedia.com/books/practical-empathy/) contains a blog and additional content. The book's diagrams and other illustrations are available under a Creative Commons license (when possible) for you to download and include in your own presentations. You can find these on Flickr at www.flickr.com/photos/rosenfeldmedia/sets/.

FREQUENTLY ASKED QUESTIONS

How are you using the word "empathy?"

This book is not about the kind of empathy where you feel the same emotions as another person. It's about understanding how another person thinks—what's going on inside her head and heart. And most importantly, it's about acknowledging her reasoning and emotions as valid, even if they differ from your own understanding. This acknowledgment has all sorts of practical applications, especially in your work. This book explores using empathy in your work, both in the way you make things and the way you interact with people. Chapter 2 introduces the nuances among different types of empathy.

Can anyone learn how to be empathetic?

Curiosity about people is key to the empathetic mindset. A core inquisitiveness about other people's thinking and experiences is necessary. This curiosity can be something that starts small and grows over time. People who have received constant positive feedback for speaking about themselves might have a hard time learning to be curious about other people. In addition, people who are used to solving other people's problems (like a doctor) will have a difficult time turning off their deductive thought process in order to absorb more detail through listening. These criteria are discussed in Chapter 2.

How should I train to increase my empathy skills?

Practice listening to people every chance you get. Practice shutting down your inner voice so that you can hear more clearly and recognize when you need to ask more to really understand something. Practice recognizing your own emotional reactions, so you can dissipate them before they distract you too much from listening to others. In Chapter 4, there are some practice exercises to try out.

What do I look for in a candidate when I need to hire an empathetic person?

Look for core curiosity about other people. Look for the intent to support others better. These are discussed in Chapter 2. Additionally, look for the ability to listen, silence the inner voice, and dissipate reactions, as explained in Chapter 4.

How can I train my team to be more empathetic?

Teach your team how to listen deeply and show them how to practice by doing it yourself or with them, over lunch or during meetings. Additionally, the experience of working through the stories and creating summaries is a powerful way to improve listening skills. Summaries are explained in Chapter 5.

How do I clearly convey insights I've gained via empathy to my peers and decision-makers, even across departments?

Repeat the clearest stories you've heard. When you open your mouth, other people's voices will come out. An important part of your job is to "pollinate." Get these perspectives out among the people of your organization who need them. Suggestions how to do this appear in Chapter 6.

How does empathy improve my interaction design skills?

Empathy doesn't directly help you lay out the steps of how a person uses your solution. Empathy is knowledge that lines the inside of your skull, awaiting the random creative inspiration. When the inspiration happens, your collected knowledge serves as a foundation to support, hone, or disprove the idea. Empathy helps your team decide on the overall direction and flow of what you are making so that it supports the intents of a specific set of people. Chapter 6 shows how this works, and Chapter 8 addresses it in the context of your organization.

CONTENTS

FOREWORD

As an entrepreneur and product designer, I care about empathy for very practical reasons. The best product managers, designers, product teams, and leaders are experts at practicing empathy. They are able to understand and learn from the perspective of the other person—who might be a customer, a user of a product or service, or a stakeholder in the process of creating it. And their products somehow feel "just right" or "intuitive" to a million different individuals. This is no accident.

Indi Young's book is a practical manual for practicing empathy, which is a skill, not an innate talent. Empathy is a mindset that can be learned and improved with practice. There are best practices, techniques, and tools that help you get your own ego out of the picture and focus on what things are like from another person's perspective. It is not easy to do really well, but it is worth doing really well! And Indi's book shows you how to do it.

Practical Empathy offers advice on how to practice an empathetic mindset toward other people involved in the conception, design, or implementation of a product. I find this to be particularly relevant in today's modern high-tech company, where extreme time and resource pressures mix with high expectations and under-constrained choices. Companies respond by hiring all-star teams of diverse players, working cross-functionally with other teams. Somehow, these herds of high-tech cats need to purr together, like the cylinders in a Jaguar sedan. It doesn't happen with top-down, military style command and control. It happens with collaboration, persuasion, negotiation, constructive compromise, and distributed decision-making. This requires empathy for the other person in all of these conversations.

Many organizations also turn to measurement and statistical analysis to try to make evidence-based decisions and align all the players involved in product development around objective outcomes. This is a perfectly sensible thing to do, but not in isolation. Quantitative data-driven processes optimize for collective outcomes and ignore that which is not measured. Qualitative data-driven processes optimize for individual outcomes and embrace the messy complexity of case studies and user perspectives. How can we get usable data from this "softer" source to make decisions about qualitative things like user interfaces? Indi's book offers valuable techniques to gather the subjective data of empathetic observation and conversation, and analytical tools to make sense of it.

—Tom Gruber, product designer and co-founder of Siri

INTRODUCTION

I wrote this book to give people an easier way to bring perspective to their work. At first, my intent was to help everyone make more mature things, nuanced and customized to reflect how different people think. I wanted people to discover new vocabulary for talking about what they make instead of using technology as a basis of description. And I wanted to broaden people's thinking to include services, processes, policies, and written content in the definition of "things you make." Bringing perspective to what you make all hinges on understanding the person you are supporting—understanding his thinking process as he fulfills an intention that is much larger than whatever means he is using to achieve it.

I had introduced this concept in my book about mental model diagrams, but I saw some people get bogged down in the process of building the diagram and in the vocabulary. (I used the word "tasks," which is too action- and product-focused for the kind of reasoning and reactions I was capturing.) The power of the diagram is to compare how people think to how you support them (see Figure I.1), and getting both sides of the diagram into shape was sometimes more than people wanted to do. While most of the stories I heard were about people who were successful with the diagrams and have made them

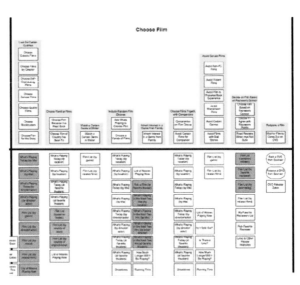

FIGURE I.1

This movie-goer mental model diagram depicts thinking, reactions, and guiding principles above the horizontal line, grouped into towers by concept, and the features and services that a movie production company provides in support of each tower below the line.

repeatedly, I was worried about those who turned away. I told them there were shortcuts—that a diagram could be roughed out in a couple of intense days. Even though I would say this, not everyone embraced it. The people I worried about returned to techniques that focused on the thing being created and the experience of it by a "user," rather than on the person's larger cognitive and emotional context.

So I decided to grab the top part of the diagram, break it down, and focus on getting the word out about that. Listening is such a transformative skill. It is what allows you to develop empathy—to understand someone's inner landscape. Listening is what brings new perspectives. Never mind all the details. If you only listen and never write any details down, your mind will still retain about 30% of the new perspectives. That's enough to work with. That's enough to counterbalance a confined focus on what is being created. Any time you listen—plugging directly into a person's train of thought—it sets off a cascade in your brain, which, a few days later, causes you to see your work in a slightly different light.

As I wrote this book, I also discovered that listening to develop empathy has another use in what people do at work. So many people

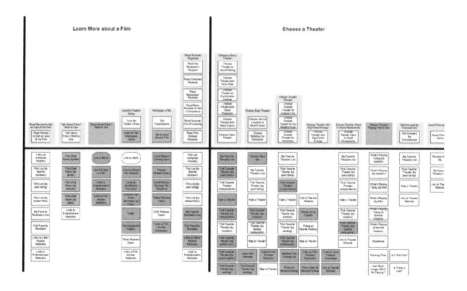

battle every day with others they work with. Communication isn't clear, goals get blown out of proportion, egos tangle, concepts seem to conflict, etc. Collaborating with peers, coaching direct reports, understanding where your leaders are coming from—all of it is transformed by listening. So I decided to include a few scenarios about listening to the people you work with, which involves setting aside your own agenda entirely. Setting aside your own agenda is also the key to spreading what you've learned to the people you work with. It all links together.

Listening and developing empathy with all the people related to your work will give you a strong foundation of understanding. It will influence the decisions you make, the words you use, and your very attitude.

Add empathy to the way you
already do your work.

CHAPTER 1

Business Is Out of Balance

Here's the situation: most organizations are out of balance, but they don't know it. They do know that creative ideas are important. They know that strong collaboration forges better solutions and execution. But they still scramble to make both creativity and collaboration produce a more reliable return on investment in their product development and operations. No matter how many agencies and management consultants they hire, no matter how many promising experts they bring on board, things still don't go as beautifully as they hoped.

At a certain level, you know opportunities exist to enrich what you are creating and improve how people in the organization work together. But you've seen how reality gets messy and how your leaders don't always make the decisions you'd hoped for. Improvements you're trying to make for the good of other people aren't happening. You hear similar stories from your peers, and it seems to all come down to one reason: you're not being heard. You keep repeating what you know to be important, but nothing seems to improve.

A significant portion of this failure can be assigned to each person in the organization, from the very top of the hierarchy to the very bottom. Each person has, to one degree or another, a cloudy awareness of his own motivations and guiding principles. Each person has, in one way or another, failed to explore the deeper currents of reasoning in the people around him. Each person has spoken but failed to listen. It's true that awareness of other people's perspectives allows you to develop much stronger solutions together. Knowing someone's perspective involves *empathy*. Empathy requires *listening*. It is empathy that will have a huge impact on how you work. It's empathy that will bring balance to your business.

Data and Analytics Take Priority

Within most organizations, attempts to improve the services they create seem to follow traditional production and efficiency paths. Leaders use metrics to measure their confidence in a new idea so that business decisions are "based on solid data." Analytics prove that specific things happened, like the findings from dating organization OkCupid about *stated* age preferences versus *actual* contacts with potential dates. "35-year-old heterosexual men ... typically search for women between the ages of 24 and 40 ... yet in practice they rarely contact anyone over 29."[1] The president of the company decided to use the data sitting on his servers "for direct introspection,"[2] making conclusions about behavior by inference rather than by asking about people's actual guiding principles. (And simultaneously adding to the heated debate about companies using member data for any purpose they choose.)

Organizations declare themselves to be "data-driven," "evidence-based," and even "engineering-focused" as a way of showing how reliable they are to potential investors, partners, shareholders, and customers. These numeric measurements tell the story of what is happening in myriad ways. There are rings and rings of data around what has happened, when it happened, how it happened, and who participated from where. For example, Amazon has mountains of quantitative data about who purchases what and when. They also have the resources to pick through these numbers and find places where they want to ask, "Why? What were those people actually thinking?" And they can go ask those people. But not many organizations have the resources or the awareness to go find out the story of why.

What is the story of *why*?

The story of why is about the purpose a person has for doing something. For example, you don't just open a savings account to save money for a big holiday. You open a savings account because you're thrilled that you're finally in the right position to actually follow your dream, the one you had since you were 12, about studying ancient cultures and going on an archaeological dig. Your motivation feels much different than saving for a car or a house. A house and a car are things your culture says you ought to save for; this holiday is your passion, not anyone else's. You make your contributions to the account differently. If the bank only knew why you were saving, it could give you better support than deducting a set amount from each paycheck or making an announcement on social media for you to try to pressure you to "own your goal." If the bank knew, it could maybe allow an external service to move $15 from your checking account to your savings account based on a trigger, such as when you favorite any articles with the word "archaeology" in them. But the bank is stuck in its own perception of saving money for a goal.

---

1 Rudder, Christian. *Dataclysm: When We Think No One's Looking*. New York: Crown, 2014. (Rudder is president of OKCupid.)

2 Natasha Singer, "OkCupid's Unblushing Analyst of Attraction," *New York Times*, September 6, 2014.

Product strategy may have something to do with technology, but it has *everything* to do with people. Comprehending the human half of the picture is one of the major aspects missing from providing any service or product. The human half of the picture is an underlying foundation for creativity.[3] It defines areas you can explore. Unfortunately, you can't force creativity down a rational, numeric path; it is well documented as a right-brained activity. This is why organizations need to understand the story of why. If the bank only knew why you're doing what you're doing, it could use your story as real data to get creative about supporting you—and others driven by a similar passion.

Immature Data Practices

Contemporary uses of data are immature. People within organizations try hard to apply the numeric data they have collected, but their approaches don't have the benefit of decades of experience. Part of the reason is that people are still struggling to grasp in a useful way the overwhelming amounts of data that the digital world can produce. So because of this, many organizations slide back into a comfortable routine. Instead of leaps of progress, they tend to focus on linear improvements in transaction conversion and on copying what other organizations are doing. Instead of exploring the actual reasons behind the numeric trends, organizations simply twist numeric metrics into hyperbole to grab market attention.[4]

Additionally, when organizations try to leverage the data they have to affect the human side of the picture, they often take a childish approach, improving the links to social media, for instance, but not focusing on anything deeper. It's like the desire to show that "we use the data" is more powerful than using the data for real.[5]

---

3   Other elements supporting creativity include things like physical environment, peers, imagination, and downtime for the brain (the latter being part of the explanation for why so many people think up good ideas in the shower).

4   Berkeley researchers did a study of which kinds of cars stop for a pedestrian waiting at a particular crosswalk. They reported that "wealthy people have less compassion toward others." This result was based on the correlation between the original cost of the car and the percentage of all the cars that day that did not stop. Correlation is not causation. No work was done to hear stories from the drivers. The researchers don't even know if the drivers were actually the owners of the cars. http://psychology.berkeley.edu/news/how-rich-are-different-poor

5   I hear this frustration expressed by many folks. Jonathan Baker of SAP uttered this particular sentence, and it sums up the emotion succinctly.

People at your organization may think the story of why is not as solid as numeric data. Most professionals understand that people are not reducible to metrics and numbers, yet when they introduce qualitative methods to balance out the numbers, they get push-back.

Here's why they're wrong. Unfortunately, the common assumption is that the qualitative and quantitative data are two extremes of the same spectrum (see Figure 1.1). Qualitative is suspected as a weaker, less-defined extreme. Quantitative and qualitative are not opposite ends of the same spectrum. They are two different spectrums.[6] They measure two different things. Quantitative measures the numeric amount of something, and can run from estimates at one end of the spectrum to detailed calculations on the other. Qualitative represents patterns in data, often in terms of words instead of numbers, and can run from guesses at one end of the spectrum to detailed depictions at the other.

Humans describe their reasoning with words. Reasoning cannot be measured with numbers. But it can be analyzed for consistency and affinity. Qualitative and quantitative data are two different parts of the whole story. There are other systems in addition to these two, such as an emotional spectrum, or the spectrum of a certain demographic such as age. To use only one spectrum is to paint a picture with only one color.

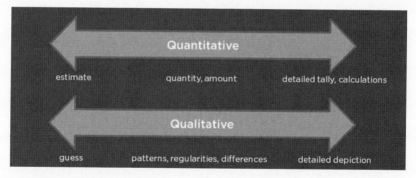

FIGURE 1.1
Be ready to recognize if people in your organization perceive quantitative data as "solid" and qualitative data as "soft." Both have valid and soft ends of their spectrums.

---

6 Patrick Whitney, Dean of the Institute of Design, Illinois Institute of Technology, in his keynote presentation at User Friendly Conference 2012, Beijing. Patrick also referenced Albert Einstein, who was attributed to have said, "Just because it's something you can't count doesn't mean it doesn't count."

Abuse of Scientific Terminology

Another aspect of this fascination with the solidity of numbers is that people use (and abuse) scientific-sounding words in order to persuade people. Half the time people don't even realize they are using the words for persuasion. This vocabulary has been used for decades in marketing, news, health, sports, and in the way that executives and leaders speak. People within organizations toss off phrases like, "Studies show that …" and "Our tests verify …." Rarely do these phrases actually indicate that a scientific process was followed. There was no hypothesis, no experiments disproving or supporting the premise, no alternative measurements and comparisons, no looking up similar studies that other people have done. No one outside the group tries to reproduce the results to make sure the conclusion is correct. So it's not really science, but the vocabulary is pervasive. People respond to it.

For instance, if a decision-maker at your organization feels uncertain about the potential of an idea, he might ask you for "proof"—for numbers to clarify what decision he should make. You might conduct a quick survey, which feels scientific. Yet the results are only used to make people feel comfortable about heading in a certain direction. The results usually favor whatever you intend, of course, because it's devilishly hard to write a survey that doesn't represent your own perspective. Moreover, you're converting people's answers into numbers and ignoring the words. These converted numbers simply hoodwink everyone into feeling more confident.

Once you're aware of it, you'll hear and see scientific terminology everywhere. For example, as shown in Figure 1.2, a gym attracts customers with the phrase "sports health science." The phrase seems to come directly from the name of a collegiate degree. There is probably legitimate science going on in that industry, with studies about professional sports players and about sedentary populations, but you don't go to this gym to access that science. You go to access a professional who will motivate you to work out.

FIGURE 1.2

A gym is a gym—but this one is *better*, because it gives you "sports health science!"

Constrained Collaboration

Collaboration is hindered by differences in perspective. Divisions within larger organizations often measure and describe components of the same data differently, which makes their interpretations different and confusing. Not only is the picture half-painted, but the part that does get painted is represented with dissimilar vocabulary and diagrams. The marketing group wants everybody to make decisions based on the customer marketing segments they've defined, but the software folks want to pursue features in support of the search analysis they've done. Everybody's busy explaining to each other how their perspective works—their definitions, vocabulary, and methods. Or worse, they're ignoring other people's perspectives or questioning their intelligence. Collaboration is not the smoothly oiled process you wish it could be.

Self-Focused Progress

Organizations forget to look beyond their own activities. In contemporary organizations, the energy of product strategy, creativity, and collaboration is focused only on efforts directly related to the things an organization delivers, rather than looking at people's intents or purposes. Decision-makers try to understand employee, stakeholder, and customer "needs" and "requirements." They focus on ways to get ahead of past failures and competition, how to keep up with external demands, or to predict future trends. They hope for a disruptive innovation.[7] All these efforts are directed at how well the organization collaborates, puts together, and presents its *solutions*. They're all derived from industrial roots.[8]

Decision-makers have very little solid knowledge about context beyond what they deliver. What's going on in somebody's mind? What is his motivation and larger purpose? There is very little effort put toward understanding the people involved. A product (or market) strategy was put in place a while ago and seems to be a foregone conclusion. Organizations feed their creative process with metrics about how things work currently. Only small groups that are actively attempting to pivot away from a direction that has not provided the expected returns take the time to look beyond the horizon of what's in place already.

Lack of Listening

Anytime moving parts are out of alignment, it causes friction, which can shake your organization apart. Friction causes wear and tear on the people who work there and the people you serve. Everyone genuinely wants to prove his worth, impress people with great ideas, or just plain old fix things. Most of the time professionals are so busy trying to contribute their ideas and get other people to change that

---

7 The Wikipedia entry on disruptive innovation defines it as a new idea that causes a whole existing market to quickly lose customers, like when jets displaced train and ocean liner travel. http://en.wikipedia.org/wiki/Disruptive_innovation

8 "We're still designing our services in the same way we designed our manufacturing production process," Dave Gray, presentation "The Connected Company," agiledesignprinciples.com. "Technology has been imitating the industrial age to make more stuff, faster and better." Patrick Whitney keynote presentation, User Friendly Conference 2012, Beijing.

they don't realize they've spent zero time understanding those other people and listening to them. No one is listening because everyone thinks others need to understand what he has to say. Consequently, understanding what is going on in other people's minds is the first step toward counterbalancing the fascination of numbers and familiar perspectives.

FIGURE 1.3
Everyone genuinely wants to contribute. No one is listening because everyone is talking at once.

What Makes a Person Tick?

Most organizations don't try to understand people—there is too much variety and uniqueness in what drives decisions. For example, the reasons people get involved in a local civic issue depend upon the issue, the location, and the person. There could be 50 different reasons, which is far too many to address for any one organization—so the organization predefines two opinion groups to keep it simple and then assigns people to those groups.

- Open the park to professional baseball, for the benefit of local kids and local restaurants.

- Keep the park nonprofit so the constant crowds, litter, parking, or noise won't despoil our neighborhood.

It turns out, though, that if you explore all the 50 reasons, there is more correspondence between the concepts than you'd expect. The deeper guiding principles that drive decision-making tend to cluster into just a few types of intentions.

- I intend to provide a service to a group, like kids, who need something more.
- I intend to make my neighborhood a safer/quieter/cleaner place to live.
- I intend to do something locally that will serve as a model and contribute to something larger.
- I intend to increase my property value.
- I intend to increase the profits to local small businesses so they can thrive.

You can see how the intent to increase my property value could be held by people in both opinion groups. Debating about how to fulfill some of these intentions might make better civic engagement than simply polarizing around the two opinions and whipping up a media firestorm.

The difficulty lies in getting past everybody's habit of emphasizing opinions and using them to represent a person's inner reasoning. This habit might be rooted in a mode of "hurriedness"—the desire of industrial cultures to accomplish more within each day.[9] This desire results in quick but mostly shallow interactions that rely on assumptions you make about what the other person means. This speed also relies on shared cultural references or stereotypes that, even if meant in jest, symbolize philosophical stances. Saying "This project is on the road to nowhere; we are time-constrained, as always," could actually mean you feel threatened by your manager, that you feel powerless to fix the process, or that you got distracted by a more exciting topic and didn't actually make any progress on your assignment. Not many people take time to find out what's underneath a statement like this, so communication remains shallow.

---

9 Phoebe Sengers, "What I Learned on Change Islands," *Interactions Magazine*, Volume XVIII.2 March + April 2011, interactions.acm.org/archive/view/march-april-2011/what-i-learned-on-change-islands1

Some cultures fixate on preferences and opinions, letting those stand in for deeper reasoning. Other cultures tend to hold opinions more privately because it is considered impolite to thrust your opinion up against someone else's publicly. When you look beyond preferences and opinions, you get a much more practical understanding of what a person is thinking. Going deeper than assumptions and opinions is what's called *empathy*.

What does a deeper practical understanding look like for a business? Take the example of a service organization supporting external customers—say an airline and its passengers. Studying how someone books a flight, for example, uncovers the mechanics of looking for the cheapest, least painful routes. In Figure 1.4, they all appear to be painful.

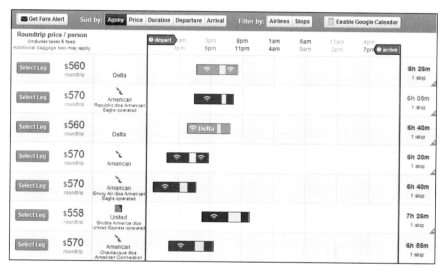

FIGURE 1.4

Looking on Hipmunk for a flight from San Francisco to Louisville reveals that there are no direct flights. "Agony" already.

Going deeper and understanding why someone books a flight reveals some important reasoning. Based on many sessions listening to passengers, say the airline has divided them into four different sets of motivations and approaches, two of which are those who want the trip to be as quick as possible, and those who want to extend it. Some people feel obliged to take trips, while others look for opportunities to travel. Some people want to squeeze in other things to accomplish on the day they fly, get home to their toddlers as soon as possible, or sleep in their own beds. Others enjoy adding a weekend to a business trip to explore someplace new or to visit family. Although this behavior does change for certain individual trips, it appears to be a norm for most trips.

Passengers in both behavioral groups are forced to spend time searching for different combinations of flights, dates, and times that might fit their intentions. In Figure 1.5, passengers have to look through an overwhelming 369 options on Kayak to find that one magical, perfect flight. Additionally, since the destination requires a connection, passengers must consider the circumstances of each of the connecting airports. For example, the first five flights connect at airports known for delays during thunderstorm or snow season. In Figure 1.6, the airline encourages passengers to poke around on other dates just to make doubly sure there isn't a better option.

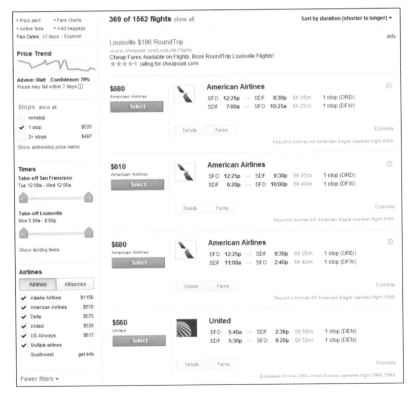

FIGURE 1.5

Sorted by duration, there are still an overwhelming 369 number of options on Kayak to look through.

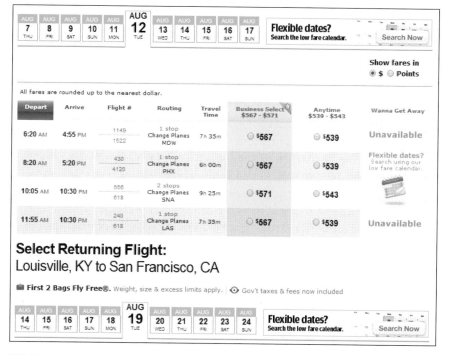

FIGURE 1.6

Southwest has a reasonably small number of options, but urges you to poke through the dates just to be sure there isn't a better option.

Next, the airline reaches for its quantitative data: of these two behavioral types, which one spends the most money with the airline? Is there a reason to postpone working on a solution for one of the groups, in order to prioritize for the other? Maybe there's a dip in spending during the winter on the part of the quick-trip types, or maybe they tend to take short-haul trips with no connections, which means less money spent overall.

In this example, it turns out there is no such correlation. The airline won't prioritize one group over the other, but it will aim to create different approaches to better support each group.

To better support the quick-as-possible type of passenger, you could let him enter the dates and times of his must-attend events or places, either at home or away, and then offer three or four options instead of hundreds. This filtering down to just a few options based on the passenger's situation and habits is what travel agents used to do for people. Additionally, you could show options outside your own service that fit the criteria better. Currently, none of the airlines or booking services shows you options that combine flights from airlines that are not partners. Even if there's a chance of missing a connecting flight due to a delay, if the trade-off is a six-hour layover between flights, many people would be willing to take that risk.

Looking beyond the flight reservation tool itself allows the service organization to see opportunities to support someone more intimately. Imagine helping a passenger look at a custom list of options (including partners in rail and local ground transportation, say, for the trip-extenders) based on his travel philosophy, past trips, and activities scheduled on his calendar. Likewise, a different organization, like a bank, would be able to use the knowledge to aim its offers to earn miles toward free travel only to the trip-extenders. Sending these offers to the quick-trip types only telegraphs the message that the bank does not understand or care about this group's motivations and reasoning. This additional data about what makes different people tick deeply affects the kinds of changes you make in your service offering.

Rebalance Your Organization with Empathy

Believe it or not, it's not such a hard problem to get past the surface level. Once you get down to the deeper principles and reasoning that guides people's actions, you can find solid, repeating patterns. These patterns will help you address specific concepts you had not acted in support of before. You can double-check a decision that was previously only based on numeric metrics. And your interactions with people can be improved. Communication with the intent to support your deeper understanding of someone can advance collaboration—both in your work group and across divisions. Empathy will play a role in rebalancing your organization's clarity of purpose in the post-industrial, post-digital frontier creative age. *You* can be one of the people who pauses more often to listen and understand.

Taking time to be curious
about people is key
to the empathetic mindset.

Empathy Brings Balance

Going deeper than assumptions and opinions in your understanding of people is powerful. If your organization is captivated by metrics, empathy will balance out the numbers. Being honest about what you don't know, being interested in the simpler underlying philosophies that make people tick—these characteristics are what can catalyze your creativity and your collaboration.

Empathy Is Not What You Might Think

At first, most people seem to think that empathy is about showing warmth and kindness, or at least tolerance, toward another person. People think empathy is "to walk in someone else's shoes," to put themselves in that person's place and embrace or excuse his behavior. This is not what empathy is about. Not exactly.

Empathy is a noun—a thing. Empathy is an understanding you develop about another person. Empathizing is the use of that understanding—an action. Empathy is built through the willingness to take time to discover the deep-down thoughts and reactions that make another person tick. It is purposely setting out to comprehend another person's cognitive and emotional states. Empathy then gives you the ability to try on that person's perspective—to think and react as she might in a given scenario. In Figure 2.1, you see the division between developing empathy and applying it.

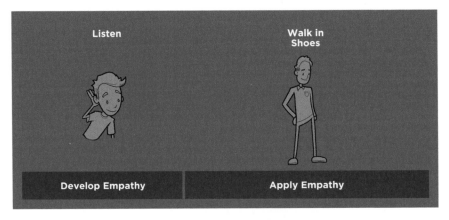

FIGURE 2.1
You can't apply empathy until you've developed it by listening deeply to a person.

This use of empathy is what most people confuse with empathy itself. People try to act empathetic—to take someone's perspective, to walk in his shoes—without first taking time to develop empathy. This leap is problematic when it comes to your work. You end up with business decisions based on expectations about how others are reasoning, not based on knowledge. There are some notable examples that have resulted in loss of market share and stock value:

- **BlackBerry:** The organization Research in Motion focused only on corporate phone users who, presumably, would not be interested in viewing video or games on their devices. It persisted in shipping devices with physical keyboards, which it thought corporate "email warriors"[1] required (see Figure 2.2). Not until too late did it realize that corporate users loved the larger screens on the touch devices, and the physical keyboard forced the Blackberry screen footprint to be too small. This is a case of applying empathy based on an assumption, rather than on actually spending time doing the work to develop empathy.

PHOTO CREDIT: SCOTT BALDWIN, @BENRY

FIGURE 2.2
The late model Blackberry Bold still had a physical keyboard.

1 Sam Gustin, "The Fatal Mistake That Doomed BlackBerry," *TIME Magazine*, September 24, 2013.

- **Windows 8:** Microsoft made the assumption that all customers would want the same "familiar" interaction experience on their phones, tablets, laptops, and desktops, and that the focus of the experience would be on touch rather than mouse. However, on laptops and desktops, the larger touch-enabled targets result in greater mouse movement between clickable items (see Figure 2.3). Additionally, the experience emphasized photos, video, social media, weather, appointments, and the apps took up the whole screen. The enterprise customer who wanted to get real work done was forced to break through this crust down to the desktop where her spreadsheets, documents, drawing, and collaboration tools existed. Again, this was a case of applying empathy based on the assumption that customers need familiarity across devices, and that touch would be a prevalent input method in scenarios where people needed to be productive.

FIGURE 2.3
Win8 on a touchscreen laptop means the user switches between tiles and desktop, between direct-touch and mouse.

- **Netflix:** In 2011, the movie-rental company's CEO made a unilateral decision to focus on streaming and carve the physical DVD delivery business into its own separate company. His assumption was that DVDs were already on the way out (see Figure 2.4), and apparently he expected the separate company to quietly fade away over time. His poorly worded announcement caused furor among customers who already enjoyed access to both streaming and DVDs—the selection of movies available by streaming was more limited than what was available by DVD, and customers were being asked to pay a higher separate fee for each service. Not only that, but the services each required their own account and movie queue. The company lost 800,000 subscribers, and their stock price lost three-quarters of its value.[2] This example demonstrates not only a lack of developing empathy for, say, customers who did not enjoy reliable broadband access, but actually shows an inability to think from the customer's standpoint at all. This decision was wholly focused on the future of the business, not on the customers.

DON'T BITE THE HAND THAT FEEDS YOU. ESPECIALLY IF IT HAS HAIRY KNUCKLES.
HAPPY HALLOWEEN!

FIGURE 2.4
A red Netflix DVD envelope with a seasonal message.

---

2 Greg Sandoval, "Netflix's Lost Year: The Inside Story of the Price-Hike Train Wreck," *c|net*, July 11, 2012.

Hundreds of other less acute examples result in missed opportunities and wasted budgets.

Leaping to action without a solid comprehension of the people you are affecting causes all sorts of mayhem, both internal and external to organizations. This leap gets made because of confusion between empathy and empathizing, because of the hue and cry in business to be lean, quick, agile, and minimally viable, and because guesses and assumptions about other people are so believable.

Empathy is built by dropping into a certain mindset when the opportunity arises to gather knowledge. If someone you want to understand has the time, you take it. You drop into a neutral frame of mind, try to discover the deeper reasons behind what she is saying, and shut down your own thinking and emotions (see Figure 2.5). This neutral mindset will bleed into many aspects of your creativity and interactions at work. You will be able to empathize more reliably, using a solid comprehension of the people around you. You will be able to clarify the reasons why you choose to do something so that it better supports people's underlying reasoning. You will be able to see the initiatives of others and selflessly work in support of them. This neutral mindset is what enables both developing empathy and applying empathy. It's an empathetic mindset. And you will drop into it and out of it occasionally—it's not a constant state of grace that you must struggle for.

The empathetic mindset does not mean you have to feel warmth for another person. The words "understand" and "comprehend" do not mean "adopt" or "agree with." At times, you may not feel comfortable with the other person's thinking, but that will not affect your neutral mindset. You will just be aware of it and able to consider and adjust for her way of thinking.

Developing empathy is straightforward. It takes certain listening skills to get past the layer of explanations, preferences, and opinions to get at intention and why. These skills help you set aside your own preconceived notions and listen in a whole new way. And these skills take practice, but they are not difficult. The only struggle with developing empathy is that it takes time. Not a lot of time, but time, nevertheless. You will need to make and defend that time. You may need to help others at your organization recognize the return on investment of that time.

So empathy is not about warmth and kindness. It's about listening. It's about having a frame of mind that is curious about the deeper flow of people's thinking.

FIGURE 2.5
Empathy is built through the willingness to take time to discover the deep-down thoughts and reactions that make another person tick.

Variations on Empathy

In psychology literature, the type of empathy defined in this book is called cognitive empathy. This kind of empathy is one of several variations.[3] Each of these variations is about *developing* empathy—the part where an understanding of someone else builds in your head.

- Mirrored empathy: Some neuroscientists posit that when a test subject sees face, mouth, and hand movements of a source subject, that test subject's brain fires in a similar manner to the source's brain. Emotional transmittal occurs as a result. Speech patterns are often mirrored, too, which is a useful way of establishing rapport. Mirror neurons could also be the pathway for learning and for the basis of a host of other mental abilities, although there is some controversy about this.[4]

- Emotional empathy: In this form of empathy, the other person's emotion leaps the gap between you, causing you similar feelings and memories. It's like a strike of lightning. This emotional resonance is called *affective empathy* in psychology literature. Affective means emotional, so you can also call it *emotional empathy*. Emotional empathy is not limited to face-to-face encounters; it can arc between you and an actor in a movie or a character in a book, like in Figure 2.6.

- Empathic concern: If you have sensed emotional empathy, you might then develop an array of reactions having to do with the situation the other person is in. These feelings may lead to some act on your part toward the person.

- Personal distress: If you realize something distressing is happening to someone else, you either experience a sharp moment of the same distress, or you try to ignore or "un-see" the person's predicament. Imagine seeing a friend chopping vegetables and cutting herself, or witnessing a stranger loudly cussing at another person in the grocery store.

---

3 Daniel Batson reviewed psychology publications and found at least eight different uses of the word empathy. See his chapter, "These Things Called Empathy," in the book *The Social Neuroscience of Empathy*, edited by Jean Decety and William Ickes, MIT Press. Daniel Batson is Professor Emeritus at the University of Kansas.

4 Ramachandran, V.S. *The Tell-Tale Brain: A Neuroscientist's Quest for What Makes Us Human.* New York: W.W. Norton & Company, 2011.

- Cognitive empathy: This is the kind of empathy discussed in this book. Cognitive empathy is purposely discovering the underlying thoughts and emotions that guide someone else's decisions and behavior.

- Self empathy: Self empathy is turning your purposeful discovery inward, to learn how your own mind reasons and reacts. It is the subject of many spiritual practices, meditation, as well as the subject of exploration between a patient and a psychotherapist.

People also mix up empathy with sympathy. *Sympathy* also has varying definitions, but most often is characterized as offering someone kind words, usually when that person is feeling distress.

FIGURE 2.6
Books, movies, and games rely on mirrored and emotional empathy for you to identify with the characters.

Empathy Becomes Your Practice

You have your expertise; there is a certain way you like to approach your work. Your approach is your practice—the enactment of your profession. This characterization of the word "practice" is meant to clarify that the empathetic mindset is a skill that is suitable to add to your existing set of professional skills. The empathetic mindset can be approached as a structured discipline, which makes it a tool for anyone wanting to advance his career. It will enhance your strategic thinking, your creative process, and it will transform your ability to work together with others.

Who is likely to learn empathy? The capacity for empathy develops naturally for most people during childhood.[5] For some children, empathy comes more intuitively than others, as is true for the little girl in Figure 2.7, who, a decade after this photo was taken, still demonstrates intuitive ability to develop and apply empathy. Almost every child eventually comprehends that other people can think and feel differently. So, for adults, "learn empathy" might not be the correct phrase to use. A better phrase might be "adopt an empathetic mindset." Who is likely to be good at that?

Curiosity about people is key to the empathetic mindset. Even if you're an introvert, you might still be full of curiosity about people. Adults who possess a certain degree of self-absorption will have trouble practicing an empathetic mindset. Society likes to joke that there are certain fields of work which tend to attract more egocentric individuals, where they can receive competitive recognition (e.g., doctors, lawyers, game designers, advertisers, entrepreneurs, and financiers). But even if there's some truth to that correlation, it does not mean narcissism is true of everyone in that role. Being in a certain field does not cause or imply narcissism. Another type of person who may have difficulty adopting an empathetic mindset is one who has trouble with language or does not think verbally.[6] So much of communication between people comes from language, so linguistic skills are probably key to developing an empathetic mindset. In truth, most people can develop an empathetic mindset if they have at their core inquisitiveness about other people's experiences.

---

5 "Kids under six are in the 'preoperational' stage, a key characteristic of which is egocentrism. They can't fully empathize with others until they're around seven." Debra Gelman, author of *Design for Kids: Digital Products for Playing and Learning.* New York: Rosenfeld Media, 2014.

6 See also articles by Temple Grandin and about the work of Charles Bliss.

FIGURE 2.7

Nicole, 3 years old, reads a story to the orange corn snake (which you can see hiding under the fake rock in the terrarium) before "putting it to bed" for the evening. She believes the snake wants the same kind of comfort that a story gives her at bedtime. The example demonstrates very early development of curiosity about the thinking of other people (or rather, reptiles).

Whether you have an intuitive talent for empathy or not, you will still need to practice. Here is the second characterization of that word. You will need to continually practice, to get better and to maintain your skill. Just like a football player or a rock climber or a pianist, you will need almost daily practice with your empathetic mindset. The empathetic mindset is not a method with a list of steps you can refer to as needed. It's not about following a procedure and taking notes. It's about understanding another human being, mind-to-mind, without any accessories (see Figure 2.8). It's about thinking of other people first before making decisions. Practice will bring you confidence so that you can develop a strong empathetic mindset.

FIGURE 2.8
The empathetic mindset is about understanding another human being, mind-to-mind, without any accessories.

Exhibit Understanding Instead of Competence

Here is a story about an emperor in ancient China. He attracted many people to his court who wanted to share the distinction of shaping the future of the land. These court members vied for the emperor's attention, competing with each other to suggest more magnificent ideas and, incidentally, to bring trade and projects to the people who were his friends outside of court. The emperor bestowed his consideration on one after another court member, intrigued with each person's idea because it matched his desires precisely and seemed so clear and risk-free. But either the idea produced disappointing results, or the court member would be defamed by others before the idea came to fruition.

One member did not present any ideas to the emperor. Others chided him for his lack of inventiveness and warned that he would soon lose his position. Instead, he sat and listened to the emperor talk about the prosperity of his people and the increase in production from the land. One afternoon, the court and the emperor were discussing a project to build a structure that would reach into the heavens, taller than any other building in the land. Court members were arguing about how to engineer the foundation and how they might build each level to support the next. To the surprise of everybody in the room, the quiet member spoke up.

"The purpose of this building is to allow the emperor to be closer to the heavens?" Yes, everyone agreed; the purpose is to symbolize the glory and wisdom of the emperor.

"The purpose is to build a structure that will demonstrate the wisdom of the emperor?" The emperor gazed fixedly at the member and nodded.

The member continued, "The emperor's wisdom has provided a fertile land for his people, who grow in numbers. Let him extend the lands which are fertile and increase the magnitude of trade by constructing the largest canal and reservoir system for irrigation and transportation."

The room was silent, shocked by the mundane idea. But a smile spread slowly across the face of the emperor as he thought through what the idea would mean for the prosperity of his people. He pointed to the member and said, "This is what we will build instead."

Within all sorts of organizations, many people are thinking, "I want a seat at the table so I can tell the leaders what they should really be doing." With an empathetic mindset, you let go of that need to change others or to demonstrate your competence. Instead, you listen for the deeper reasoning and philosophies within other people. Together, you explore these deeper currents and work out better solutions. Because you've formed an unequivocal understanding of purpose, the results are more likely to be marvelous.

The empathetic mindset starts with you.

FIGURE 2.9
Focus on supporting a person to achieve a purpose, rather than on making an impressive statement.

Empathy can help you
think outside the box and see
past the fog of details.

Put Empathy to Work

When bringing the empathetic mindset into your practice at work, you need some structure. You need ways to explain the difference between developing and applying empathy, as well as how it hooks into your existing development and collaboration processes. You also need pointers on how to reach out to people and how to set up an interaction where you can earn their trust. These appear in this chapter.

Later in this book, there will be tips and guidelines, as well as some vocabulary to use, which will help you establish your capability to empathize with people in your work. The guidelines will also help you measure your improvement at applying empathy. The overall idea is to move beyond the lightning-strike epiphany form of emotional empathy, shifting to cognitive empathy, and turning that into harnessed electricity that helps your own practice, and that of your organization, run smoothly and dependably.

Development Cycles

When you create something, every project you undertake goes through cyclical stages of development as you mature and polish the ideas. One common representation of these stages is the Think-Make-Check cycle.

During the *Think* stage, you brainstorm ideas that could either become a solution or influence the solution you already have. All the details of developing the idea occur during the *Make* stage, even if that development is simply a sample or sketch of an idea.[1] Then in the *Check* stage, the idea gets poked and prodded not only by the potential end customers (commonly referred to as "user research"), but also by the creators and the stakeholders.

Typically, organizations focus hard on their development cycles, which means they spend most of their energy cycling around the ideas they have. The Think-Make-Check cycles all rotate around ideas or solutions. They do not rotate around people. If you're going to balance out that focus on solutions, you can introduce a separate

---

1 Agile and Lean processes try to put a perimeter around development, so that not too big a chunk is attempted before testing it with the people it is designed to serve. Both Agile and Lean are predicated on principles that make people a focus. The Agile manifesto focuses on "Individuals and interactions … [and] … Customer collaboration." Lean principles optimize "value from the *standpoint* of the end customer." See also agilemanifesto.org and www.lean.org.

cycle of empathy that focuses on people and their purposes. In other words, study the problem space in addition to the solution space. This person-focused cycle will rotate more slowly than your development cycles, but you will always be reaching out, every few months, to people to add more understanding to your repository. Your understanding of the deeper reasoning and broader purpose of people will feed your empathetic mindset. Then it will be present in your mind during brainstorming—or during the Think stage of the cycle around an idea (see Figure 3.1).

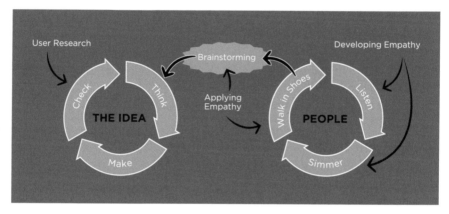

FIGURE 3.1

When you create something, each project cycles around an idea you want to bring to fruition. Adding a parallel cycle that focuses on people brings much greater depth to your brainstorming.

The Stages of Developing and Applying Empathy

As you set out to adopt an empathic mindset at work, it might help to envision a set of stages that you pass through. The stages group into two parts: developing empathy and applying empathy. You cannot apply empathy before you have spent time developing it. You need one to do the other.

Developing empathy starts with listening, of course. Then there's an optional period after listening during which you think through, reread, or summarize the things you heard. You let the information simmer, if you like, allowing yourself to build a much deeper, richer understanding of what you heard.

"User research," where a solution is checked to see if it works for people who might "use" it, is one of many types of research done by organizations to guide decisions. There is also "market research," where organizations seek to understand consumer preferences and trends, so they can craft their offerings to suit, or alternatively, where organizations assess the viability in the market of a new idea. There's "competitive research," where an organization seeks to understand the capabilities, both present and future, of competing organizations to possibly win customers away from them.

All the research projects that organizations perform, no matter which type of research it represents, tend to fall into two categories: evaluative or generative. Evaluative research seeks to judge how well something works for a person. Generative research seeks to collect knowledge about a person or context or market that can serve as a foundation for creating new ideas. The kind of empathy defined in this book is *generative research*.

Solution Focused

Generative
perspective and empathy to create ideas

Stakeholder Interview
Participatory Design, Co–Design
Observation–as–Participant
Experience Strategy Map
Mental Model Diagram (bottom)
Kano Analysis/Graph
Use Case, Scenario
Personas (in scenarios)
Swim Lanes
Wireframes
Prototyping

Evaluative
whether it serves the intended purpose

Usability Testing
A/B, Multivariate Testing
Remote Testing
Eye Tracking
Competitive Analysis
Content Inventory/Audit
Focus Group
Benchmarks, Comparison
KLM, GOMS
Heuristic/Expert Review
Cognitive Walkthrough
Physical Ergonomics Review
Accessibility Study
Search Analytics

FIGURE 3.2
Most exploration in support of creative work is solution-focused. There is a need for more person-focused exploration.

For those who are involved with evaluative and generative research, there is one more distinction you may be interested in. Typically, all research that has to do with a "user" is really about the solution or idea that will be "used." The word "feedback" disguises a similar meaning—feedback is hearing things about the solution or idea. Rarely does generative research focus only on a person, paying attention only to the person's thoughts and reactions and purpose, as opposed to looking for opportunities to fit your idea into his life. Person-focused generative research is a powerful sibling to solution-focused research, telling you the story of why someone makes decisions the way he does (see Figure 3.2).

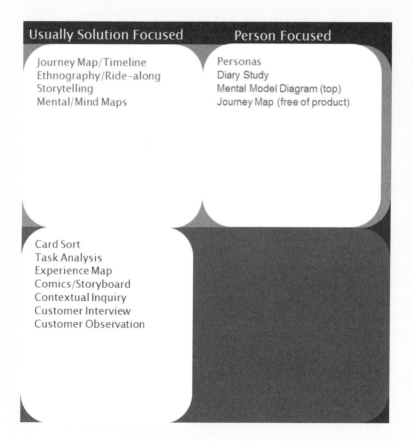

Usually Solution Focused

Journey Map/Timeline
Ethnography/Ride-along
Storytelling
Mental/Mind Maps

Person Focused

Personas
Diary Study
Mental Model Diagram (top)
Journey Map (free of product)

Card Sort
Task Analysis
Experience Map
Comics/Storyboard
Contextual Inquiry
Customer Interview
Customer Observation

Applying empathy starts, in some contexts, by looking for patterns of thinking and decision-making and aggregating them across a whole set of people. In other contexts, like when you are trying to move fast, you skip this stage entirely. Either way, the next stage is to step into a person's shoes and try on his reasoning processes (see Figure 3.3). The exercise is meant to help you decide about something you are creating, for example, a new hiring process for your division, or about some interaction with a person in your work, like when you face someone who seems to be obstructing your progress. These stages will be detailed in the next few chapters of this book.

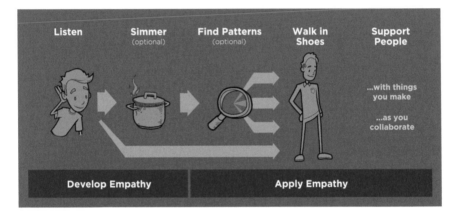

FIGURE 3.3

The two parts of an empathetic mindset, developing and applying empathy, are distinct. They are intended to guide your decisions and actions in the things you create and the interactions you have with others.

Empathy is, ironically, often used for persuasion. In marketing, in politics, in the media—the purpose of understanding someone else is often to induce a change in his beliefs or behavior. This is not the only use of empathy. Empathy is also used to encourage growth or maturity in young people, teaching them to respect perspectives that are different than their own. Empathy is used to affect subject, tone, and vocabulary to be able to initiate communication with a person. Additionally, empathy is used literally to act like someone else, imagining how to behave in a series of situations.[2] However, the application of empathy that has impact on your work is to *use it in support of someone*. Empathy in support is being willing to acknowledge another person's intent and work with it, morphing your own intent because of the empathy you developed for the other person.

While you are developing empathy, what you learn is evergreen. People's reasoning patterns do not change overnight. Patterns do not change as a result of tools and technology—mostly, only the frequency and speed of achieving a purpose changes. The knowledge you are building will last, foreseeably, the length of your career. Because the knowledge is long-lived, you don't have to hurry through cycles of building it. It will always be there, and you can always add to it—even if a couple of years have passed by.

NOTE WHEN NOT TO SAY THE WORD "USER"

The word user is directly tied to a product, service, process, policy, or content. Indeed, you might say "patron," "reader," "guest," "patient," "passenger," "member," or any number of other nouns to describe a person who takes advantage of what you have created. It's fine to use these nouns when applying empathy. But when you are in the stage of developing empathy, the person has no relation to what your organization delivers. The person is simply a human you are trying to understand more deeply. When developing empathy, avoid saying any of these "user" nouns. Say "person" or "human" or even the individual's name instead.

The Logistics of Listening

There is a lot of flexibility with empathetic mindset listening. Here are some pointers. First, even though the word "listening" implies hearing someone, you can "listen" via written words. As long as you write back questions about what was written, to get a better idea of what lies underneath, writing is a perfectly acceptable way to "listen."

---

2 Some movie directors emphasize character depth over story. Director Mike Leigh gives no script, no lines to his actors—just a character sketch. *Happy Go Lucky* is one of his movies created like this. Director Drake Doremus created *Like Crazy* with a one-month rehearsal of the actors as the characters. See also: John Anderson, *New York Times*, "Free Rein to Play Free Spirits," Oct 21, 2011.

Ordinarily, though, you will listen by hearing someone speak. This listening implies synchronous speech, because you'll want to go back and forth with the person in a conversation—talk, dig deeper, talk, dig deeper. You will connect with this other person face-to-face or remotely (see Figure 3.4).

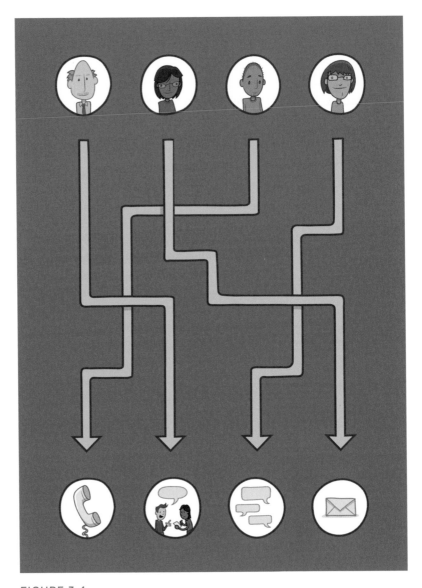

FIGURE 3.4
There is a lot of flexibility with listening. You can even "listen" via written words.

A Formal Listening Session

You can either drop into listening mode informally, during interaction you are having, say, in the hallway with a peer, or you can purposefully set up a time to listen to a person. If you set up a formal time, refer to the session either as "a conversation" or "a listening session." The word "conversation" implies that dialogue will go back and forth, which isn't strictly correct. But it's a common enough word to describe what you are doing. Use "conversation" when setting up a session with the other person. In your own head, use the phrase "listening session."[3] This phrase attempts to get at the intention of following that person's words, rather than contributing to the dialogue.

Just don't think of a listening session as an interview. The word "interview" is so overloaded that when another person hears you say it, he is likely to be thinking of a different thing.

For formal sessions, you will necessarily go through the process of finding the right people to set up appointments with. You'll want people who are comfortable describing things—skip those people with single-word answers. When you set up the appointment for a spoken listening session, you can mention the scope in advance, as well as any details you'd like about the project or your organization and the purpose of the listening session. For written sessions (essays with Q&A follow-up), you can do the same in your written introduction.

A formal listening session lends itself well to being recorded. A recording will make the next stage much easier, because you will be able to go back over what was said if you can't remember it all. If you have a transcript made from the recording, then it is even easier to go back over what was said, and even search for certain words that you remember, so you can reacquaint yourself with the context. According to law in many countries, you must get a person's permission to record the session. Verbal permission can be documented in the recording itself, for convenience. If a person unexpectedly does not want to be recorded, follow his wishes without complaint. You will still remember enough from the session for it to be worthwhile to continue.

---

3 The design research agency STBY uses the phrase "empathic conversations" to refer to this kind of listening session. www.stby.eu/2012/09/03/empathic-conversations/

Empathy Is Not an Interview

The word "interview" has so many meanings. Each interview type has a distinct purpose and format. So, to keep from confusing the meaning further, simply avoid the word, even though it's true that listening sessions are a *type* of nondirected interview for the purpose of developing empathy.[4]

The English word "interview" can mean:

- A meeting between a potential employer and a candidate during which the employer tries to assess the skills and attitude of the candidate, and the candidate tries to decide if the job and coworkers are right for him

- A conversation that a radio, TV, studio, or panel host conducts with a guest for the purpose of entertaining or educating an audience with the guest's answers

- The format in which a reporter collects statements from an expert or witness, with the potential to be used as quotes in his material

- The discussion a detective has with an expert or witness to gain an understanding of what might have truly occurred

- The way a design researcher understands how a person uses a product, service, content, or process, for the purpose of judging how well the item functions

- One format for a psychotherapy consultation

---

4 In my book about mental model diagrams, I called the listening sessions "interviews" or "nondirected interviews," but the message about *understanding a person as a human* seemed to get lost among all the other definitions for "interview."

If you are engaged in a formal listening session via remote connection, you also have the opportunity to invite your peers to listen in. Again, according to law in most countries, you are required to ask permission for these peers to listen. These additional listeners must remain muted, but they can be connected via chat or shared documents for learning purposes or to exchange comments about what is said. Sometimes, when a person agrees to the additional listeners, he may be hesitant with his answers. Rarely does this hesitation last more than five minutes into the session, since the remote listeners are easily dismissed from his mind.

Why Is a Remote Connection Okay?

Among researchers, remote listening causes disagreement. Ethnographers lean toward observation as a superior method. Usability researchers cry out, "Get out of the building! Get in front of your users!" The prevailing sentiment is that in-person sessions provide richer information, because of body language and physical context. In-person sessions are praised as a way to help you understand little details a *study participant* wouldn't think to report, or might feel inclined to report differently. For developing empathy, though, remote listening is equally as good. Depending on your own habits and comfort level, as well as the other person's topics and context, remote listening is sometimes better than in person.

Remote listening is acceptable because of the phrase "get in front of your users!" For evaluative *research*—where people are using a solution or service—yes, get out into the real world. It can really deepen your understanding.[5] However, developing empathy is not focused on a solution or experience. In a lot of cases, it's not even research. It's just you building your knowledge about how another person thinks his way toward a purpose. Even in the cases when you're developing empathy with your organization's customers—and it can be called research[6]—their purposes are much larger than any solution or experience your organization provides. You are exploring concepts with a person that have little to do with the use of any particular thing. The details reside completely within the person's head, because you're only exploring *within* the boundaries of the mind. Remote listening is perfect for connecting mind-to-mind.

Sometimes, it actually helps to have a remote connection. If you don't feel like you have control over your facial expressions, or if you are afraid that aspects about the other person might inadvertently prejudice or distract you, then a remote connection will conveniently

---

5 See also Steve Portigal's book, *Interviewing Users*, especially "Be Selective About Social Graces," page 21. New York: Rosenfeld Media, 2013.

6 Although, in terms of listening sessions and developing empathy with customers, a better word than "research" is "exploration."

hide all of this.[7] Additionally, since you cannot see the other person's environment, he will automatically include more descriptions of how his world affects his thinking in his speech. These descriptions give you more material to dig into. Because he is free of your potentially unskilled body language, he will feel free to honestly discuss his thinking on sensitive subjects, such as health or finance. Often, the person will undergo a little self-discovery as he makes sense of his interior thoughts in a way he hadn't thought of before. The distance created by a remote connection gives you and the other person both space to be comfortable.

One at a Time

The only inflexible rule about listening is that you should listen to one person at a time. You need to concentrate, and you need time to explore this person's deeper reasoning. And, if the other person is going to tell you his innermost thinking, he needs the opportunity to develop trust in you. There can't be other people telling their stories at the same time. If there are other people, as is true for focus group studies, some members of a group will end up deferring to others, or even adopting their beliefs in an effort to fit in or make the session go more smoothly. You really don't want group dynamics interfering with the depth of conversation you want to reach. So, listen to only one person at a time.

No List of Questions

If you have any familiarity with interviews, even if you reach back to your school journalism days, you know that great effort is put into forging a predetermined list of questions. But a listening session is not an interview. Throw out your list of questions. Don't put effort into researching what topics might come up. Any forethought will distract you from what the other person will tell you. You'll do fine without a list, just like you do well enough without a list of questions at conferences, parties, and weddings. There are more guidelines about how to run a formal listening session without a list of questions in the next chapter.

---

7 This applies to remote video connections, such as Google Hangouts, Facetime, or Skype, where you might consider turning off video and sticking to just the audio portion of the connection.

As a life coach, Zô De Muro has 25 years of experience listening to his clients as they explore how to make big changes in their behaviors to reach their health goals. Over time, he has come to the conclusion that the Observer Effect[8] is most obvious in face-to-face sessions. "Clients often want to please coaches, so they'll say things to elicit a positive reaction," Zô says. To minimize the Observer Effect, Zô prefers to conduct client sessions by phone. The client can then focus on himself. "Having the physical distance allows clients to open up more completely."

Zô has learned to pay close attention to a person's voice. He listens to inflection, tone, speed, pitch, cadence, and pauses. Each has a spectrum of meanings—especially the silences. "Altogether, listening closely to a client's voice tells me tons of information."

Lastly, Zô wears hearing aids as a part of his everyday life. He embraces the technology that boosts a hearing aid when on a call. "When I'm on the phone, I can crank up my headset, so I hear nuances that would be lost in person because of ambient noise."

---

8 The Observer Effect implies that the person watching a thing, an event, or a person slightly changes the way it behaves. Zô's favorite explanation of it has more of a physics bent to it, but the concept also applies here. http://www.grc.nasa.gov/WWW/k-12/Numbers/Math/Mathematical_ Thinking/observer.htm

Keep It Simple

The best part about listening is that you don't have to be "a good facilitator" or a "skilled interviewer" to develop empathy. It's more about just being yourself, in curiosity mode. Kids can do it. What it takes is the ability to let go of your own thoughts and really absorb what you hear.

So, now you're ready to get into the details of this new way of listening. The next chapter contains a lot of tips. Give yourself space to take it all in; your mind will take a few months to absorb everything. Practicing these tips in tiny daily listening sessions will help you gain competence.

Developing empathy means focusing only on the peaks and valleys of what the person tells you, nothing else.

A New Way
to Listen

To develop empathy, you need to understand a person's mind at a deeper level than is usual in your work. Since there are no telepathy servers yet, the only way to explore a person's mind is to hear about it. Words are required. A person's inner thoughts must be communicated, either spoken aloud or written down. You can achieve this in a number of formats and scenarios.

Whether it is written or spoken, you are after the inner monologue. A recounting of a few example scenarios or experiences will work fine. You can get right down to the details, not of the events, but of what ran through this person's mind *during* the events. In both written and spoken formats, you can ask questions about parts of the story that aren't clear yet. Certainly, the person might forget some parts of her thinking process from these events, but she will remember the parts that are important to her.

A person's inner thought process consists of the whys and wherefores, decision-making and indecision, reactions and causation. These are the deeper currents that guide a person's behavior. The surface level explanations of how things work, and the surface opinions and preferences, are created by the environment in which the person operates—like the waves on the surface of a lake. You're not after these explanations, nor preferences or opinions. You're interested in plumbing the depths to understand the currents flowing in her mind.

To develop empathy, you're also not after how a person would change the tools and services she uses if she had the chance. You're not looking for *feedback* about your organization or your work. You're not letting yourself ponder how something the person said can improve the way you achieve goals—yet. That comes later. For developing empathy, you are *only* interested in the driving forces of this other human. These driving forces are the evergreen things that have been driving humans for millennia. These underlying forces are what enable you to develop empathy with this person—to be able to think like her and see from her perspective.

This chapter is about learning how to listen intently. While the word "listen" does not strictly apply to the written word, all the advice in this chapter applies to both spoken and written formats.

This Is a Different Kind of Listening

In everyday interactions with people, typical conversation does not go deep enough for empathy. You generally stay at the level where meanings are inferred and preferences and opinions are taken at face value. In some cultures, opinions aren't even considered polite. So, in everyday conversation, there's not a lot to go on to understand another person deeply. To develop empathy, you need additional listening skills. Primarily, you need to be able to keep your attention on what the person is saying and not get distracted by your own thoughts or responses. Additionally, you want to help the speaker feel safe enough to trust you with her inner thoughts and reasoning.

There's virtually no preparation you can do to understand this person in advance. There are no prewritten questions. You have no idea where a person will lead you in conversation—and this is good. You want to be *shown* new and interesting perspectives.

You start off the listening session with a statement about an intention or purpose the person has been involved with. In formal listening sessions, you define a scope for the session—something broader than your organization's offerings, defined by the purpose a person has. For example, if you're an insurance company, you don't define the scope to be about life insurance. Instead, you make it about life events, such as a death in the family.[1] Your initial statement would be something like, "I'm interested in everything that went through your mind during this recent event." For listening sessions that are not premeditated, you can ask about something you notice about the person. If it's a colleague, you can ask about what's on her mind about a current project.

Fall into the Mindset

How often do you give the person you're listening to your complete attention? According to Kevin Brooks, normally you listen for an opening in the conversation, so you can tell the other person what

---

1 If you're a researcher, it helps to know that listening sessions are a form of generative research that is person-focused rather than solution-focused. Thus, it's easy to remember to keep them from dwelling on how solutions might work for people. See also the sidebar "Types of Business Research" in Chapter 3.

came up for you, or you listen for points in the other person's story that you can match, add to, joke about, or trump.[2]

It feels different to be a true listener. You fall into a different brain state—calmer, because you have no stray thoughts blooming in your head—but intensely alert to what the other person is saying. You lose track of time because you are actively following the point the other person has brought up, trying to comprehend what she means and if it relates to other points she's brought up. Your brain may jump to conclusions, but you're continually recognizing when that happens, letting it go, and getting a better grip on what the speaker really intends to communicate. You're in "flow," the state of mind described by Mihaly Csikszentmihalyi.[3] You are completely engaged in a demanding and satisfying pursuit.

It's a different frame of mind. You don't want to be this focused on someone else all the time—you have to do your own thinking and problem-solving most of the time. But when needed, when helpful, you can drop into this focused mindset.

Simply Absorb and Understand What You Hear

If you've conducted interviews in a professional role, you may think of yourself as a good listener. But consider what your brain is doing during those interviews. Often, professionals remain in an "interviewer" frame of mind, continuously analyzing what is being said and comparing it to what they need and what others have said. In certain circumstances, interviewers may be trying to represent an organization or make a good impression. Additionally, professionals may be frantically considering ideas for the next question. All of this brain activity will interfere with the kind of listening you want to do for empathy. You want your mind to be empty, without thought, so that the speaker's thoughts can fill you up. The only current going through your mind is continuously checking if you are making an assumption about what is being said.

---

2 This was my epiphany from the UX Week 2008 workshop by Kevin Brooks, PhD; http://boxesandarrows.com/files/banda/user-experience-week/UXWeek08-Brooks.pdf. Sadly, Kevin passed away from pancreatic cancer in 2014.

3 Mihaly Csikszentmihalyi, widely referenced psychologist and author, *Flow: The Psychology of Optimal Experience*, New York: Harper Collins, 1991, and *Finding Flow: The Psychology of Engagement with Everyday Life*, New York: Harper Collins, 1997, plus four other book titles on Flow. Also see his TED Talk and YouTube presentations.

Explore the Intent

Developing empathy is about understanding another human, not understanding how well some*thing* or some*one* at work supports that person. Set aside this second goal for a bit later. For the time being, shift your approach to include a farther horizon—one that examines the larger purposes a person is attempting to fulfill.

The key is to find out the *point* of what the person is doing—why, the reason, not the steps of how she does it. Not the tools or service she uses. You're after the direction she is heading and all her inner reasoning about that direction. You're after overarching intentions, internal debates, indecision, emotion, trade-offs, etc. You want the deeper level processes going through her mind and heart—the things that all humans think and feel, no matter if they are old or young, or you are conducting the session 500 years ago or 500 years in the future. These are the details that will allow you to develop empathy. Collecting a shallow layer of explanation or preferences does not reveal much about how this person reasons.

To remind the speaker that you're interested in answers explaining what is going on in her mind and heart, ask questions like:

- "What were you thinking when you made that decision?"

- "Tell me your thinking there."

- "What was going through your head?"

- "What was on your mind?"

If you suspect there might be an emotional reaction involved in her story that she hasn't mentioned yet, ask: "How did you react?"

Some people ask, "How did that make you feel," but this question can introduce some awkwardness because it can sound too much like a therapist. Additionally, some people or industries eschew talking about "feelings." Choose the word that seems appropriate for your context.

Avoid asking about any solutions. A listening session is not the place for contemplating how to change something. Don't ask, "Can you think of any suggestions …?" If the speaker brings up your organization's offering, that's fine—because it's her session. It's her time to speak, not yours. But don't expand upon this vein. When she is finished, guide her back to describing her thinking during a past occurrence.

Make Sure You Understand

It is all too easy to make assumptions about what the speaker means. You have your own life experience and point of view that constantly influence the way you make sense of things. You have to consciously check yourself and be ready to automatically ask the speaker:

- "What do you mean?"

- "I don't understand. Can you explain your thinking to me?"

Keep in mind that you don't have the speaker's context or life experience. You can't know what something means to her, so ask. It takes practice to recognize when your understanding is based on something personal or on a convention.

Sometimes, you will probe for more detail about the scene, but there's nothing more to say, really. These kinds of dead-ends will come up, but they're not a problem. Go ahead and ask this kind of "please explain what you mean" question a lot, because more often than not, this kind of question results in some rich detail.

You don't need to hurry through a listening session. There's no time limit. It ends when you think you've gotten the deeper reasoning behind each of the things the speaker said. All the things the speaker thinks are important will surface. You don't need to "move the conversation along." Instead, your purpose is to dwell on the details. Find out as much as you can about what's being said. Ignore the impulse to change topics. That's not your job.

Alternatively, you might suspect the speaker is heading in a certain direction in the conversation, and that direction is something you're excited about and have been hoping she'd bring up. If you keep your mind open, if you ask her to explain herself, you might be surprised that she says something different than what you expected.

It's often hard to concede you don't understand something basic. You've spent your life proving yourself to your teachers, parents, coworkers, friends, and bosses. You might also be used to an interviewer portraying the role of an expert with brilliant questions. An empathy listening session is completely different. You don't want to overshadow the speaker at all. You want to do the opposite: demonstrate to her that you don't know anything about her thinking. It's her mind, and you're the tourist.

Toddlers Aren't Embarrassed

Another aspect of keeping your mind free of assumptions is to ask:

- "Why's that?"

- "What do you mean by that?"

Get into the toddler frame of mind. Toddlers are really comfortable with letting their brains feel empty. They don't have the same internal reasoning going on that adults have. Toddlers just absorb what is being said. As they encounter ideas that aren't clear or are a new use of words, they ask for an explanation. They ask "why?" in succession. They are not embarrassed about not knowing. Mimic a toddler's empty mind: focus on whether you understand what is being said. Of course, don't take the toddler why-why-why approach to the point where it becomes annoying. After all, most of the actual toddler-adult conversations end with the adult saying in exasperation, "Because I said so!"

Sometimes it's not a matter of assumptions, but that the speaker has said something truly mystifying. Don't skip over it. Reflect the mystifying phrase back to the speaker. Ask until it becomes clearer.

Don't stop at your assumption. Teach yourself to recognize when you've *imagined* what the speaker meant. Train a reflexive response in yourself to dig deeper. You can't really stop yourself from having assumptions, but you can identify them and then remember to explore further.

Another way to explain this is that you don't want to read between the lines. Your keen sense of intuition about what the speaker is saying will tempt you to leave certain things unexplored. Resist doing that. Instead, practice recognizing when the speaker has alluded to something with a common, casual phrase, such as "I knew he meant business" or "I looked them up." You have a notion what these common phrases mean, but that's just where you will run into trouble. If you don't ask about the phrases, you will miss the actual thinking that was going through that person's mind when it occurred. Your preconceived notions are good road signs indicating that you should dwell on the phrase a little longer, to let the speaker explain her thought process behind it.

Listen for Three Components

It gets easier after years of experience to recognize the kinds of things being said while listening to the torrent of ideas flowing from a speaker during a session. But for now, all you really need to track is whether you are discovering the speaker's deeper reasoning.

The things you are looking for are different than in colloquial speech. The things are also different than what you seek in most professional interview and research formats. For example, a job interview might focus on what the other person's skills are and her problem-solving ability. A talk show host, for instance, will try to elicit stories and secrets that will amuse or provoke the audience. In a usability study, you look for difficulties, complaints, work-arounds, wishes, conjecture, and so on. Empathy is more neutral. To develop empathy, you listen for these three things:

- Reasoning (inner thinking)

- Reactions

- Guiding principles

If you imagine the speaker's stories are a current flowing past you, you'll eventually get skilled at watching what flows by in the depths, so to speak. You want to be able to identify these three types of things. *There goes an emotional reaction … That's some thinking, right there … Oh, there's a guiding principle, finally. Let me ask more about that, and skip over that crust of explanation floating on top.* (See Figure 4.1.) Recognize what is helpful to developing empathy. This recognition will also help you identify the places where you need to dig behind a statement to understand the reasoning better.

Inner Thinking or Reasoning

Inner thinking is literally what is going through your mind. It's the reasoning beneath the action you take, every decision you make, and every statement you say. The words "beneath," "behind," and "deeper" all convey the idea that you don't want to stop and accept the first thing a person says. Usually, the way someone starts a story is with an explanation. *This happened, and so then I did this.* With such a statement, you have to guess why the person did that thing. If you end up with all the facts of a story, but none of the reasoning, then you do not understand the person at all. You've only got guesses.

FIGURE 4.1
Learn to go deeper than the crust of typical conversation and discover the reasoning, reactions, and guiding principles flowing underneath.

Reactions

A reaction is a response to a situation or stimulus. In listening sessions, usually the reactions you hear about are emotional, in response to a specific circumstance the person is describing. Reactions are important to identify because they go hand-in-hand with reasoning. Sometimes an emotional reaction to some external event sets off a chain of reasoning. Sometimes an internal thought process causes an emotional reaction. Reactions run underneath a person's behavior. If you don't find out what is flowing through someone's heart, you have missed a chunk of the story.

Contrary to expectation, people have an easy time talking about their emotional reactions. They come out readily, because they are tied in with thinking, and because they are not usually big earth-shaking emotions. They're ordinary emotions, like frustration, hope, or trust.

Note that an emotional reaction is defined by a specific stimulus. A series of similar stimuli can create a mood, such as elation or disgust. A mood is important to explore so that you can get at the underlying stimuli and reactions. However, if you only know about the overarching mood, it won't help you understand how that person thinks.

Guiding Principles

A guiding principle is a philosophy or belief that someone uses to decide what action to take, what to choose, how to act, etc. It is a philosophy that a person can apply to many events in her life, and she subconsciously relies upon it to help her behave in a manner consistent with her standards. Examples of guiding principles are "avoid disturbing the people around me" and "there should be a place for everything, and everything in its place." Discovering guiding principles is important to developing empathy because they illustrate the foundation of someone's perspective. It is much easier to walk in that person's shoes if you know her guiding principles and how they differ from your own. You will be able to simulate what goes through her mind during a particular experience much more faithfully.

Guiding principles are often acquired in childhood. The principles become automatic—a reflex. Because of this, it's rare to uncover a guiding principle during a session. They fly by in conversation almost unremarked. Moreover, you're apt to assume that someone's guiding principles are similar to your own, so it's natural to make assumptions about them. This is why you want to be on the lookout for them. Learning that someone's guiding principle is slightly different than your own sheds a lot of light on her perspective and gives you a handle for thinking along a different pathway than your own.

Follow the Peaks and Valleys

When you are listening to someone, keep all your brainpower focused on that person. You want to follow all the peaks and valleys and branches of the stories that person tells you, and nothing else. You want to show the person how interested you are, so that she is willing to open up. You want to urge the person to go into detail until you satisfy yourself that you understand what she means. You will avoid leading the discussion anywhere other than where she has already indicated. And above all, you will not be problem-solving as you hear what she has to say. Your own mind is only focused on listening. Here are some more details so that you can become competent at this.

Start with a Broad Topic

Begin with a broad description of what you're interested in, so the speaker selects where to go. Usually, the speaker will jump in to the topic immediately, but often she will be familiar with other types of interviews and wait for your list of specific questions. If this is the case, she will ask something like, "Where do you want me to start, exactly?" Refrain from leading her in a particular direction. A good response is, "What came to mind for you when I mentioned this?" or "What has been on your mind these past few weeks about this?" Through a little negotiation, you can get the speaker off in a direction of her choosing.

Agree with whatever she decides upon, even if it doesn't seem associated to the topic you asked about, because that is what is top of mind for her. Surprise associations like this expand your internal framework about the topic. Even Sherlock Holmes, the fictional detective, knew that he'd get greater detail and depth from a person's story if he let them choose the topic. "Just let us hear it all in your own way."[4]

Let the Speaker Keep Choosing the Direction

Let the speaker lead the conversation, and follow her closely. She will take you to all the things she wants to tell you. Let her be the tour guide,[5] and don't ask her about anything she hasn't brought up. She will get to all the things that are relevant to her if you give her time.

You should never have a list of topics to cover, so relax and see what she brings up. If it's a formal session, it might take a few minutes of encouragement to let her know that she has control. When the speaker realizes she is in charge of the session, you will hear the change in her voice and how she takes over the conversation.

Fill your mind with what the speaker is saying, and it will push aside your worry about what topic to bring up next. Listening sessions are more relaxed and stress-free than interviews. You will never have that panicked feeling of "wondering what to ask next" or "thinking up the next question" during a session. You are the serene, intensely

---

4 Quote by the character Sherlock Holmes in the book by Arthur Conan Doyle, *A Study in Scarlet*, 1887.

5 I wrote an article, "Please Pay Attention to Your Tour Guide," using the analogy of following a tour guide in Beijing, http://johnnyholland.org/author/indi-young/, October 2012.

interested, listener. Your simple job is to follow up on some of the last things the speaker said.

There might be a burning topic that you *want* the speaker to talk about, but nothing she says leads in that direction. Control yourself. Keep your own interests from interfering. There are reasons for this rule.

- If you ask about something you really want to hear about, several things can happen. You become the "owner" of the conversation, and the speaker will gladly relinquish that responsibility to you. The rest of the session will be a struggle to get her to lead the direction of the conversation again.

- The speaker may not have anything to say about the subject you bring up. Maybe it isn't something she has experience with, or it's a point of view she doesn't share. The conversation can falter, and it will take a minute to get it going again.

- The speaker will suspect that the subject is important to you, and might unconsciously engage in conjecture, fabrications, or opinion about it, in an effort to give you the information she thinks you want. None of this will be helpful. You want the speaker to illustrate how her own thinking goes and where she places importance.

Similarly, the speaker may bring up a topic that is of professional interest to you, or that you have a theory about. Resist the urge to ask questions about it that will help support your personal theory. Instead, focus on understanding her points in the most neutral manner you can achieve.

Dig into the Last Few Remarks

When faced with a session without a list of questions, most people feel a little nervous. What do you ask when the speaker finishes what she was saying? There are two directions to go:

- Ask about a topic the speaker mentioned earlier.

- Ask for more detail about a part of a speaker's story that you might have made an assumption about.

When neither of these directions is viable, then you know the session is over—don't try to push it into new territory.

Usually, the speaker will tell you a part of what was on her mind, and you'll notice that details are missing or too superficial. So it will be useful for you to make queries to get a deeper level of explanation. Often, there will be a few things to follow up on after she finishes saying something—little hooks you can use to expand the story.

You can remember most of these remarks without having to jot them down. Sometimes, however, you might need to jot one or two of them down because you suspect she won't be finished with the current topic for quite some time, and you may forget. At the start of a session, the speaker will introduce several topics. Often, she'll get to more detail about each of these topics on her own, but if you think you'll want to remind her of it later, and you can't remember all of them, jot them down. Keep these notations to just a word or two to represent the subject (see Figure 4.2).

Why avoid Monday and Friday?
Why was San Diego hard?
Why was cost an issue --reimbursed?
Smiling at the counter agent to get first class
Why stick with it?
Why wi-fi?
Delays stories?

FIGURE 4.2
Here's everything that was jotted down as a reminder to get back to during a 55-minute listening session.

Sometimes before the session really gets going, the speaker doesn't comprehend what level of detail you want. If this is the case, don't be surprised to find yourself asking for more information about every little thing the speaker says. You'll help her unfold her thoughts, and demonstrate, through your interest in details, that you want her inner monologue. The speaker usually catches on and starts providing more detail on her own.

As the session unfurls, the speaker will jump from one idea to the next. Certain details she brings up will remind her of other things, so she'll branch off into a description of those. Eventually, she'll get back to concluding her description of the original topic. You've experienced the circuitousness of a conversation like this. It's nothing new. Let it keep unfolding. Furthermore, if the speaker switches to third person, using "you" instead of "I," usually it means she is talking about her own thoughts and emotions.

Do *Not* Take Notes

A session can be informal: for example, you might run into someone in the hallway or the café. Or it can be a scheduled time to sit down and talk. And if it's scheduled, you can decide to record it.

In all cases, you will *not* take notes.

During the listening session, all your attention is on the speaker and the winding, wandering threads of her exposition. If you take notes, it will distract you from this focus. Your mind is not supposed to be doing anything but listening and trying to understand. Writing takes up valuable focus in your mind.

If you are recording the session, everything is already being captured. If you are not recording, your mind will soak up the important stuff, and you can write down what you heard later. Because of the level of concentration you achieve while listening, important things the speaker says will leave unforgettable impressions.

Most people's notes consist of observations that are the beginnings of pattern synthesis—the session is *not* the time for doing synthesis. For developing empathy, break yourself of that habit. You only get a little time with the speaker, so use all your brainpower to pay attention.

Also, don't worry—asking about details will not lead you out of scope. Think of it like mining for a certain kind of gemstone. It's okay to spend time exploring around to see where a vein leads. More than half the time, it will lead to something rich.

Use the Fewest Number of Words Possible

Use the fewest number of words that you can throughout the session. The questions you'll ask are simple and informal, like:

- "Why's that?"

- "What were you thinking?"

- "What's your reasoning?"

- "Tell me more about <her phrase>."

You don't even have to form full sentences. You can simply say:

- "Because?"

As a question, "because" allows the speaker go into more detail without you getting too specific. Let the speaker take the interview where she wants. Save yourself the effort of making a formal, well-worded question during the intensity of a session.

You'll want to make sure that your tone of voice is curious and light, rather than hard and demanding. Asking "why?" in a demanding way can sound as if you are judging the person and that you don't think she did the right thing. "So I decided to buy the cardamom ice cream for dessert." "Why?!" This type of tone makes it sound like deciding on ice cream is bad, or that the chosen flavor is disgusting. To temper your meaning, use a curious tone. Or, try saying, "What was your thinking there?"

Sometimes, you will say things in an inelegant way. It's so tempting to reword your own question so that it is clearer. Don't use the time to do this unless the speaker asks for a clarification of what you're after. Generally, the first way you say it, although not perfect, is good enough for the speaker to understand and respond. If you take the time to correct yourself, you run the risk that the speaker will get distracted while waiting for you to form your question. Instead of starting with the initial response she had to your original question, she might give a shallower answer.

Similarly, refrain from filling in silent gaps after you've asked something but while the speaker is thinking of her answer. Respect that she has to think about it and wait.[6]

Reiterate a Topic

After the speaker has finished a description, take a tiny amount of time to demonstrate that you're intensely alert to her story. Briefly reiterate what she just said, in one very short phrase—not even a whole sentence. Reflect back to her a tidbit of the content that was just revealed. Something short like, "The gate!" will work just fine. Use a word she used. "Terrifying!" Mirror her way of talking just a little bit to build rapport and show that you're on her side.

---

6 Lynn Shade, UX designer and researcher who grew up in Japan, describes how to identify three different kinds of silence: setting-the-stage, effort, and failure, in a sidebar called "Silence Abroad" in Steve Portigal's book, *Interviewing Users*, 88–89, New York: Rosenfeld Media, 2013.

You can also use a very short reiteration to test whether you have understood her correctly. She will respond if you've made a mistake comprehending her meaning. Additionally, you can use reiteration as a way to prompt the speaker to tell you a little more about the subject. "Somebody official …." If there's something more to be said, the speaker will launch into it at that point. This sort of reiteration is not supposed to be a summary of what you just heard; instead, it is just a few words or a phrase that you use to elicit a response.

Avoid Introducing Words the Speaker Hasn't Used

As a rule, stick to the speaker's vocabulary. Try not to introduce terms she has not used. If you introduce vocabulary, she is likely to change the way she normally speaks about the topic and adopt your terminology. The biggest challenge you might face is stopping yourself from unconsciously saying words that are jargon from your industry.

On a related note, you're probably already aware that leading questions are dangerous. They cue the speaker to answer in a way that she thinks you want to hear. Any question that hints at what you expect as an answer is a leading question. Usually, leading questions begin with "Do you …" or "Have you …?" Because they're so common in our everyday speech and in our media, you won't be able to completely eliminate leading questions. Don't let it make you feel anxious. If you hear yourself saying "Do you …" or "Have you …," stop mid-sentence or as soon as you can get control of your mouth. If the whole leading question comes out anyway, don't try to make it worse by taking it back. Just listen to the answer and move back into a more neutral style the next time you say something.

Try Not to Say "I"

Saying that personal pronoun "I" puts too much emphasis on your part in the listening session. You want to minimize your presence so that the session belongs to the speaker. "I want to know …." "I want you to tell me …." If you tell the speaker you want something, it's implied that you have control of the conversation. The speaker will be less likely to take the initiative to dive into a story; she will wait for you to tell her what to talk about.

Speakers are familiar with the customary interview format, and they might think you want to adhere to that call-and-response arrangement. Instead, use the pronoun "you." "You said something about …?" "What did you mean by …?"

Be Supportive

During the listening session, you will want to develop rapport with the speaker. You will want to encourage her to open up, and to do this she will need to trust you. By demonstrating that you are not judging any of her reasoning, and that you're paying rapt attention, you can earn that trust.

You're already paying rapt attention to the speaker. That devotion earns you half of what you need for a strong connection. Your support—your authentic sincerity—can earn the other half. Make this person feel comfortable; make her feel valued. When someone realizes she has your full attention, she is likely to respond to your questions gladly.

Remember a past boss you liked or a professor who was great? Even though she was in a position of power over you, you felt respected for the ideas you could contribute. You felt like you mattered to her. Chances are it was because this person knew how to listen. She knew that, because so few people really listen, it is a very powerful way to collaborate and forge a team. And, as a manager, it is a great way to encourage an individual to try her hardest to be clear and intentional in her work.

Don't Fake It—React, Be Present

Lose yourself in the speaker's view of the world. Like Yoda would say, don't *try* to be interested, *be* interested. Really, truly let yourself go—get excited by what excites the speaker. This session is not just part of "practice" or "work." It's *you*, building a new understanding of another human. Channel all your intensity toward finding out who this person really is (see Figure 4.3). Be sincere. Be present.[7]

---

7 The phrase "be present" can be interpreted as "mindfulness," being in touch with your immediate surroundings and sensations. See Thich Nhat Hanh's writing about mindfulness in Buddhism, *You Are Here*. Boston: Shambhala Publications, Inc. 2009.

FIGURE 4.3
Lose yourself in the person's view of the world.

Act human during the session; don't be a robot. React, laugh—be in the moment with the speaker. Use a reassuring tone of voice and vocal cues. "Wow!" "That's amazing!" "Huh!" Let your smile be heard in your voice. The more the speaker hears your support, the more comfortable she will be to delve into her own thought processes.

But don't overdo it. You don't want to take up the speaker's talking time during the session. Moreover, you run a slight risk of misinterpreting the emotion and offending the speaker with your response. So keep it kind of neutral. And don't start talking about yourself. Something like, "You're giving me goose bumps," is as far as you should take it in terms of referencing yourself.

Misunderstanding the emotions a speaker is trying to describe will happen. Even people who have 20 years of experience with listening sessions misunderstand what someone means. On the other hand, pretending to be interested is inexcusable. Asking for understanding and then dismissing the story and emotions that come up does nothing for developing trust. "When you ask people to open up, be prepared to listen."[8]

There is a fine line you'll need to watch for when you're developing trust from a coworker or a direct-report. If you lead that person to believe that you agree with her, but you really don't, she could feel betrayed later when she finds out. In a situation like this, you'll want to work on expressing your curiosity and understanding about this other person's point of view, instead of reflecting back a perspective that you don't truly hold. If your curiosity is genuine, if you prove that you care, she will be able to tell, and that alone will be your foundation for developing trust.

Never Switch Abruptly

Refrain from switching back to a detail a person mentioned earlier until you are absolutely certain you have explored and understood the current subject completely, from the perspective of the speaker. And never say, "Okay, great" when she finishes up a topic, so that you can ask about another detail. "That's great" smacks of your hurry to get through the session, or your need to pack in as many

---

8 Kerry Patterson, Joseph Grenny, *Crucial Conversations*, 2nd Ed., Chapter 8, "Explore Others' Paths." New York: McGraw Hill, 2013.

topics as possible. It can also sound as if you're bored or belittling what she just told you, or that you didn't pay emotional attention. Maybe what she described wasn't "great" at all, but distressing.

Now that you're aware of the "okay, great" phrase, you'll notice it everywhere. You'll hear conference hosts say it when one speaker finishes her presentation and another is introduced. You'll hear talk show hosts say it when they are trying to fit all of their questions into a defined period of time.

By the same token, do not telegraph the change in direction with phrases like "Let's switch gears," or "Now I want to ask you about …." Using these kinds of direction change phrases implies that *you're* in control of the session. You're not supposed to be; the *speaker* should be in charge of the direction of the story. Since you are only after more detail, just dive into what you want to hear about by saying, "You mentioned …" or "What was that about …" with a few of the words she mentioned. You don't even need a question after that.

Adapt Yourself to the Mood

Musicians say they can feel the mood of the audience and play differently according to that mood. Make yourself aware of your speaker so you can adapt to her a little bit. Try not to impose your own mood on your speaker.

Pick up on how the speaker is perceiving the experience of the listening session. Tune into whether she seems to think you only want to hear certain things, like only positive emotions or only logical reasoning. Encourage her to tell you the other kinds of things that looped through her mind at the time. Encourage her to relate her complete thinking process. A good listener knows that a sentence like, "It was a great experience" hides all sorts of thinking and reactions, which you will need to dig up.

A part of the mood includes the speech patterns the speaker uses. If you can, try to fall into a similar speech pattern. Mirror her style and some of her vocabulary—but not too much. Don't make her feel uncomfortable about being copied or think that she's being made fun of. For example, don't mimic poor grammar if your own grammar sticks to the rules. Just pick a few vocabulary words and phrases, and use them with a similar cadence and level of humor. Demonstrating your interest in what she has to say by copying a bit of her speech style helps establish a connection between you.

Don't Cause Doubt or Worry

Avoid saying things in a way that might make the speaker worry, doubt, or become uncomfortable. You're not saying much during the session, so it should be easy to avoid this.

"The human interaction in the interview affects the interviewees ... Consequently, interview research is saturated with moral and ethical issues."[9] You not only want to observe confidentiality with the transcripts and the results that you report, but you also want to be sensitive to what unfolds during a session, and whether the speaker is comfortable with it. You do not want to cause stress, and any changes in the way she understands herself should be self-revelations, not judgments on your part.

Be Respectful

Let the person be who she is. She needs to trust that you will not trample her sense of self, especially if she thinks you have a different way of thinking. Demonstrate that she is in charge, and that you respect her worldview. Your goal is to find out why she thinks the way she does—through lucid descriptions that you truly understand, including how she swerves around problems and slides her thinking, depending on the scenario and all the nuances of her experiences that have built up over the years. Be an expert at *curiosity* about other people—open curiosity, without analysis or assumptions. Put off analysis until you are ready to apply your understanding to design or strategy, namely, when you are trying to see patterns and make decisions for your organization.

Be the Undermind, Not the Overmind

You are not "the researcher" in the session. You have no expert role to play and no agenda to pursue. It's not about you. Your only goal is to generate trust and encourage deeper descriptions and understanding.

This part may be the single most difficult thing for people to adopt. It's hard to stop yourself from jumping to solutions. It's hard to turn off the frame of mind where you are a professional, skilled at finding themes and ideas to dive into. If you don this "research" frame of mind in a listening session, you've missed the mark. It's just the opposite.

---

9 Steinar Kvale and Svend Brinkmann, *InterViews*, Chapter 4, "Ethical Issues of Interviewing." Thousand Oaks: SAGE Publications, Inc., 2008.

Make the speaker feel confident—an expert about herself. If you act like you're an expert at deriving meanings and generalizations about people, you'll miss the chance to ask about the deeper parts of her story. If you make a comment or nod your head as if confirming a guess you'd made about the speaker, you will sound officious and kill the rapport between you. Don't let a researcher frame of mind get in the way.

Resist the Urge to Demonstrate How Smart You Are

When you meet someone new, you have a natural tendency to want to demonstrate something of your talents to that person. Circumvent your reflex to demonstrate how smart you are—to talk about your knowledge or experience. Competition will destroy the relationship you are trying to build with the speaker.

Squash your inclination to tell a speaker how things really work, as opposed to how she thinks they work. Never explain that the speaker is wrong. The speaker is always right—because this is her mind you're exploring, not her understanding of your offering, nor her knowledge of how things work in general. Whatever she thinks, it's true in her mind. This guideline assumes that you believe the speaker is being truthful. If you strongly suspect she is making things up, then just wind down the session.

---

10 A professional explains how hard it is to tell for sure that someone is lying about her story: Cordy Swope, "A Crisis of Credibility," on Steve Portigal's War Stories series, www.portigal.com/series/WarStories/

Here's another way to think about this. You're not to trespass upon the structures of her mind. If the speaker says something that's not quite correct about the service you offer, it's true for her. Squash your impulse to correct her. It's not important that she learns the difference.

Additionally, don't imply that there's another, better way of approaching things than what the speaker just told you. You'll only make the speaker feel like her reasoning is inferior.

Moreover, refrain from asking, "Are you sure?" This phrase implies that you know a better answer. Even if you don't mean it that way, it sounds too much like the way you talk to a child, encouraging him to correct himself about the deductions he made from some observation. Instead, *believe* the speaker. Ask her to tell you about the details when she first learned about the subject. Find out the reasoning underneath.

Also, if you want to share a tip or trick with the speaker that you think will make her life easier, *don't*. Avoid offering advice. The session is about the speaker, not about you or your organization. It's about her world, not yours. If you give her advice, then you're belittling her worldview. A listening session is about developing empathy. It's person-focused, not solution-focused.

Neutralize Your Reactions

Your emotional reactions can't be prevented. They're like weather, coming inexorably. At some point, you *will* react to something a speaker tells you. But if an emotion blows in on you like a rain squall, let it blow right on past you. Don't let it monopolize your attention, because then you won't be paying attention to the speaker.

Notice Your Emotional Reactions

Through your practice sessions, you can elevate your emotional literacy. If you are self-aware, then you understand when you are having emotions, what they are, and why they occurred. Recognizing your own emotions can give you emotional maturity, which allows you to realize that others can have different reactions than you do. It leads to a more open mind when trying to gain empathy with a person. Recognizing your own reactions and assumptions—before they distract you—leaves your mind open to considering foreign possibilities. You will be able to recognize when you condemn an idea or a reaction, be able to stop yourself, and then be able to spend some time investigating it instead.

Embrace Your Emotions

Meditation teacher Stephanie Noble describes a way for you to practice dealing with your reactions in her blog post, "Emotions as Honored Guests."[11] Stephanie writes, "Anger arrives at the door. Instead of saying 'Oh, God, what kind of awful person am I that I'm always so angry?' … If instead you … say, 'Hello, Anger. What brings you here today?' right at the door, the emotion may not even feel it has to come in. But never bar the door to an emotion. That kind of denial only results in emotions breaking in the back way."

11 Stephanie Noble, meditation teacher and manager of Spirit Rock Friday morning class for 10 years; "Emotions as Honored Guests," *Open Embrace Meditations* blog, http://www.openembracemeditations.com/pdfs/emotionsashoonredguests.pdf.

TIP YOU CAN'T PREVENT EMOTION

You can't realize an emotional reaction has happened until it actually happens. Don't feel embarrassed that you actually *felt* the emotion for a while first. You can't prevent emotions from occurring, but you can recognize and then ignore them.

Some people say that learning to meditate—spending time with your own brain learning its process and its habits of circumventing your intentions—helps them notice their reactions before they act. Other people learn to notice their emotions in other ways. You might need to try out different ways to learn this skill before you find a method that works for you.

None of this emotional-awareness advice is new. The founders of many of the world's religions—and some fictional religions, too—hoped to teach people to recognize and consider their own emotional reactions. Emotions are part of the human makeup, and because many humans go right ahead and speak or act based on those emotions, all sorts of excitement results. Sometimes, it can be damaging or catastrophic. It's no surprise that spiritual leaders encourage emotional literacy so that people can short the emotional circuit and use both emotional and cognitive empathy to consider other options as shown in Table 4.1.

TABLE 4.1 SPIRITUAL GUIDANCE FOR EMOTIONAL AWARENESS

Spiritual Quote	Source
"Don't give in to hate. It leads to the Dark Side."	Jedi (Yoda, *The Empire Strikes Back*)
"There is no offense where none is taken."	Vulcan (Surak, *Star Trek*)
"Fear is the mind killer."	Bene Gesserit (*Dune*)
"When anger rises, think of the consequences."	Confucian
"If one becomes angry, let him keep silent."	Muslim
"A meaningful silence is always better than meaningless words."	Hindu
"Anger deprives the sage of his wisdom."	Jewish
"Turn the other cheek."	Christian
"Holding on to anger is like grasping a hot coal with the intent of throwing it at someone—you are the one who gets burned."	Buddhist

Dissipate Your Reactions and Judgments

If you are in your own neutral emotional space, you're able to understand another person's thinking and reactions better. When you have a reaction during a listening session, you don't want to betray the fact to the speaker, because you do not want to cause her to have a reaction of her own, or let your reaction influence what she is telling you.

Don't let your negative emotional reaction get control of your thoughts or your mouth. Instead, guide any spark of condescension, disgust, shock, or anger right out of your mind. Ground it in the earth, like a lightning rod grounds lightning (see Figure 4.4).

FIGURE 4.4
Without a way to ground the lightning strike of emotion, your head might explode!

If you have trouble guiding the emotion out, make yourself take on that person's viewpoint for a moment. What would make them say or believe something? Dissipating reactions is hard to do when the speaker's reasoning gets into uncomfortable territory for you. Imagine a scenario where it makes sense from her viewpoint.[12] It's surprising how instantly free of the emotional reaction your mind will be. Practice this mechanism so that it becomes a reflex.[13]

---

12 Edmiston, Susan, and Leonard Scheff. New York: Workman Publishing, 2010. *The Cow in the Parking Lot, A Zen Approach to Overcoming Anger*, "Imagine you are circling a crowded parking lot when, just as you spot a space, another driver races ahead and takes it. Easy to feel the rage. But now imagine that instead of another driver, a cow has lumbered into that parking space and settled down."

13 See also the video, *This Is Water*, created by the agency Glossary in May 2013. The video posthumously illustrates a 2005 commencement address given at Kenyon College by David Foster Wallace, professor, novelist, and speaker. The video may still be accessible on YouTube, or you might be able to see it via this short piece on Adweek: http://www.adweek.com/adfreak/story-behind-water-inspiring-video-people-cant-stop-watching-149324.

It's all too easy to let the wrong examples guide your approach to a listening session. You hear plenty of "interviews" on radio programs and television shows. It's hard not to let them influence you. Here are a few quick pointers.

- Reporters are not good role models.
  - Don't display your point of view.
  - Opinions are not empathy (nor are they news).
  - When developing empathy, you are not after "the facts" of how something happened.
- Professional researchers are not good role models.
  - Analysis leads to brainstorming, distracting you from the person.
  - Don't think too hard.
  - Avoid demographic profiling.
  - Don't tell this speaker about other speakers.
  - Quell your excitement about an epiphany.

Harness Your Emotional Empathy

You cannot really *apply* emotional empathy. Emotional empathy is your own emotional resonance with someone, which happens during a particular instant. But you can capitalize on your ability to *notice* that you are emotionally reflecting someone else and use that connection to listen to that person and get deeper understanding.

Emotional empathy tends to strike suddenly. The other person has an emotional reaction or tells you about one he had previously, and suddenly you can feel it, too. In this situation, your awareness will help. You'll want to free yourself from the emotion itself so that you can return to understanding the other person's thinking. First, quickly recognize that you are experiencing a reaction, identify the source, and mentally step away from it—even if it's a positive emotion.

Then return to your curiosity about what underlies the other person's behavior. This curiosity is difficult to maintain if you're distracted by your own emotions.

Should you let the other person know you are sharing their emotion? Probably not. You can say something like, "Wow, I understand." The more important goal is to disentangle yourself from the emotion. Move beyond its grasp so you can focus clearly on the other person's mind again and dig deeper.

> **TIP** DON'T ASSUME EMOTIONAL EMPATHY MEANS YOU UNDERSTAND
>
> It's easy to assume that since you can identify with someone's re-action, you also share the same principles, decision-making, and thinking style. If you fall into this trap, you will stop being curious about the other person's underlying reasoning. You will lose the opportunity to develop rich cognitive empathy.

To develop empathy, you don't have to identify with any emotions. You might experience emotional empathy, but it isn't necessary. When emotional empathy happens, move past it and get back to your focused mind, so that you can use the opportunity to develop an assumption-free understanding of the person.

Practice Your Skills

Glue yourself to the topics the speaker brings up. It's easy to do, but your conversational and professional habits may make it a challenge. It will require practice. Practice means incorporating it into your everyday life and trying it out with people for a few minutes every few days or so. You'll need months of practice before these guidelines become a part of your subconscious.

Practice also helps you gain confidence. It helps you realize that people love to tell you their innermost reasoning. If you practice every time you recognize an opportunity in tiny listening sessions, it means approaching people and asking won't be as daunting as it once might have been.

The tricky part is that you do not want to think about these guide-lines while you're listening to someone. You want your mind to be empty and open to that person's thoughts, rather than full of rules to follow. So until these rules become second nature, *just forget about them*. It's more important to focus your brainpower on the other person than on the rules. For the time being, approach it more like a conversation. If you force yourself to empty your mind, you will eventually fall easily into the mindset for developing empathy. Becoming aware of your capacity of empathy is an idea that can permeate your mind quite suddenly and powerfully.

Just like practicing a sport, practicing a musical instrument, or practicing meditation, you can build your empathy skills. Little by little, you can make it a reflex. You can train yourself to reframe your thinking as situations present themselves each day. Developing empathy is not a switch that you throw.

Practice 1: Where Will You Practice Listening?

Think about your past week. Where did you go? Who was around you? In the future, which of these opportunities can you harness for impromptu, informal listening sessions? By listing these places, next time you'll recognize the opportunity to engage another person.

1. List the places you went the past week (or typically go) where there are other people around. You can list any place, as long as there are people around whom you don't constantly interact with: work, meetings, conference, grocery store, gym, bus, train, lunch line, restaurant, coffee line, even home or friends' homes, etc.

2. Scratch out the places you listed where it's usually not socially acceptable to speak to a stranger or semi-stranger, like in the elevator or the subway or a doctor's waiting room.

Practice 2: Identify Your Reaction/Assumption

Another everyday practice involves noticing when you have a reaction, when you make an assumption, when you judge, or when you classify someone. For this practice, you don't have to speak to anyone. You do have to be around real, live people, though. (Actually, TV and movies work for this exercise, also.)

As you drive, or walk through a crowd, or encounter people in a gym, or on public transit, or wherever, the game is to recognize when you have had an emotional reaction to someone's behavior or speech. Give yourself a point every time you notice your reaction. Likewise, give yourself a point when you notice you have made an assumption about what a person is doing or thinking. Also, if you realize you've judged or classified someone, give yourself a point. The points represent your awareness that you're doing it. The goal is to become aware of it, not to stop doing it.

Similar to walking 10,000 steps a day, try for 2–3 points a day for this exercise.

Practice 3: Classify What's Being Presented

You probably remember a news item or two where you were shaking your head at how "the facts" were presented. The next time you encounter such a news story, try to classify what is putting you off about the presentation. Did the reporter concentrate on opinions? Did his point of view skew the tone of the piece?

Additionally, try to identify when a report includes demographic profiling. For example, if you read something like, "Millennials who use social media become addicted and become unable to put down their phones, even late at night," rephrase it in your head in a way that neutralizes the demographic profiling. Focus on the root behavior. "People who have become addicted to social media may have a tendency to check updates late into the night."

Summary

To develop empathy, you must get past the surface level of what people tell you. This requires more attention when you listen, the ability to let go of your responses, and the presence of mind to help the speaker feel confident and understood. It requires you to let go of your need to do something, in order to demonstrate your worth. Absorb everything the other person is saying. Be passive and neutral.

This skill of listening will help you in other aspects of your life, besides work. It will help you know your mind and recognize your own emotional reactions.

WHAT TO LISTEN FOR

- **Reasoning:** Thinking, decision-making, motivations, thought processes, rationalization.
- **Reaction:** Responses to something—mostly emotional, some behavioral.
- **Guiding Principle:** Belief that guides decisions.

FOLLOW THE PEAKS AND VALLEYS

- Start with a broad topic.
- Let the speaker keep choosing the direction.
- Dig into the last few remarks.
- Use the fewest number of words possible.
- Reiterate a topic to show attention, verify your understanding, and ask for more.
- Avoid introducing words the speaker hasn't used.
- Try not to say "I."

BE SUPPORTIVE

- Don't fake it—react, be present.
- Never switch abruptly.
- Adapt yourself to the mood.
- Don't cause doubt or worry.

BE RESPECTFUL

- Be the undermind, not the overmind.
- Resist the urge to demonstrate how smart you are.
- Avoid implying or telling the speaker she is wrong.

NEUTRALIZE YOUR REACTIONS

- Learn how to notice your emotional reactions.
- Dissipate your reactions and judgments.

It's almost magical how much better you understand someone when you spend time in review.

CHAPTER 5

Make Sense of What You Heard

Listening deeply to a person allows you to develop an understanding of his reasoning and reactions—it allows you to develop empathy. The more you practice listening, the more you will notice what is being said. But perfect understanding during listening is impossible. To deepen your understanding—and consequently recognize where you could have done better in the listening session—there is another powerful technique to employ. Study what the person said.

The word "study" is meant to indicate spending time with the other person's thoughts. It's more than just a review, which admittedly often gets accomplished with only half your attention. It's reflection. You can undertake this study time in any way you like. Spending time is the best way to let the meaning and nuances soak in. Time lets you consider alternate interpretations of what was said. As is true for so many aspects of your life, giving yourself time to digest experiences and ideas always repays with a deeper perspective.

However, time is an expensive commodity within an organization. You've got to justify it. In this case, the justification is that you are sure to misinterpret statements and miss concepts if you don't study what was said. Even though it seems clear when you first hear it, even though you've got years of experience, it's guaranteed that you will misconstrue meanings. You don't want to end up working with incorrect understandings, so spend at *least* 10 minutes per person going over what was said.

Remember that this stage is still a part of developing empathy. Developing empathy is listening and identifying what flows past in the conversation, *but purposely not synthesizing or analyzing it yet*. You can't absorb how another person thinks when your own mind is active. So save the analysis for later. Allow yourself a bit of time, first to listen and then to make sense. After you do these two stages to develop empathy, then you can engage the analytical part of your brain (see Figure 5.1).

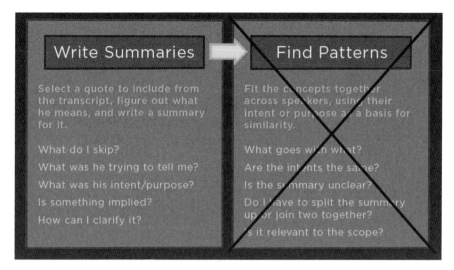

FIGURE 5.1
Writing summaries is one way of "studying" what was said. When writing summaries, stay focused on one person at a time. Don't make interpretations, deductions, or comparisons yet.

Pick Out the Concepts Each Participant Describes

You can study what was said in a variety of ways. Pick one that suits you and your circumstances.

You can study a session by discussing it with someone else at work, reviewing it in your head, or by jotting down what you remember. If you want even stronger comprehension of what was said, spend an hour listening to the recording again. Or get a transcript made of the session and read it.

You can go one step further. Gather each concept in the transcript that contributes to developing empathy: the reasoning, reactions, and guiding principles. This activity involves corralling messy, meandering dialogue. You will pick certain quotes, put them with other parts of this person's dialogue, and forge a complete idea of what the person really meant to convey. This time you spend dwelling on transcripts counts as time spent with the person. The more time you spend with him, even in review, the more you absorb his thoughts, reactions, and philosophies. You develop deeper empathy. It's almost magical how much better you will understand someone this way.

If you choose to, you can execute this quote-collection exercise however you would like. Some people make circles on printed transcripts and connect them together with lines. Some people highlight quotes in different colors to show what goes together (see Figure 5.2). Others make a spreadsheet and copy little quotes into different rows, and then combine related quotes into one row to represent one concept (see Figure 5.3). Some people even copy the quotes onto sticky notes, adding notes in the margins as more related sentences show up in the transcript. It's important to use a method that suits you, or you'll give up before reaping the benefits.

(Speaker:) Two days off work ... yay! So, I get to wind down and have a bit of a relax before the weekend starts. It's a bit of a ritual.

(Listener:) Why is relaxation important to you?

(Speaker:) I've got a really busy job. I work long hours, so if I didn't wind down, I'd just burn out. So, it's nice to be in surroundings where you are comfortable and can just relax off and *not* think about work for a couple days.

(Listener:) Why ... specifically pertaining to performances, why is this particular pub of interest?

(Speaker:) I think the music—it's known as a music pub, so it's any kind of music ... so anything goes. You could get Trash Metal one week and Rock the next and Blues or Jazz the following week, so you never quite know what you are going to get. And you can get bands from ... locally or all around the U.K., that kind of come along and do their thing. The jam session—you never know what you are going to get, because it depends on whoever decides to pitch up on that day and play. So, you get the unexpected; you get to hear some really interesting stuff.

(Listener:) The unexpected..?

(Speaker:) *Yeah*, it's nice in a way. It's nice not to know what you are going to get or what you are going to hear. You can never tell from the band name what you are going to get, so that's always quite nice.

(Listener:) Why is that important to you in a performance?

(Speaker:) If you know what's coming then it leads with a sense of excitement. If you are not quite sure what you are going to see or you are going to hear, then it's a bit

---

FIGURE 5.2
One of the many ways to gather quotes together, this example shows related concepts being collected using different font colors in the transcript. Using colors won't work for everyone, though.

ID	Quote
143	a jam session that's held once a month for all the local musicians, who just pitch up, take turns in doing their stuff. ... they'll take it in turns, so there's no formal band. You just pitch up with your instrument and play or sing or whatever. ... kind of come along and do their thing. The jam session—you never know what you are going to get, because it depends on whoever decides to pitch up on that day and play. ... Each performance is different, and you are never going to get exactly the same performance from the people. ... the enthusiasm of the people who are doing it. They are really passionate about what they do, and they really enjoy what they do. And, I really like seeing that.
143	Usually it's a really good atmosphere and good beer and good company ... it's my local pub, and it's a really nice atmosphere. It's not a chain pub or anything like that. So, it's quite a small, really friendly pub. It's a place I can go on my own without feeling awkward. I don't feel uncomfortable there ... I've been going there for years. ... it's nice to be in surroundings where you are comfortable and can just relax
143	I can have a coffee if I want to, or I can sit and have a drink. ... It's become a bit of a relaxation thing. I meet my husband off the train. It's right near my train station ... meet up with people that I know. ... I get to wind down and have a bit of a relax ... just relax off ... happy and relaxed, that's got to be a good thing
143	I meet my husband on Friday night, and we have a drink, and it marks the start of a weekend for us ... It marks the end of a working week and the start of the weekend. ... Two days off work ... yay! ... the weekend starts. It's a bit of a ritual.
143	I work long hours, so if I didn't wind down, I'd just burn out. ... not think about work ... tense and upset and stressed out
143	really good music. ... good music. ... the music—it's known as a music pub ... get bands from ... locally or all around the U.K. ... you get to hear some really interesting stuff.
143	it's all acoustics. You never know quite what you are going to get. It could be Rock or it can be Blues or Jazz ... any kind of music ... so anything goes. You could get Trash Metal one week and Rock the next and Blues or Jazz the following week, so you never quite know what you are going to get. ... you get the unexpected ... It's nice not to know ... what you are going to hear. You can never tell from the band name what you are going to get, so that's always quite nice. ... If you are not quite sure what you are going to see or you are going to hear, then it's a bit of an adventure. ... It's always going to be different, so you always get something new which is nice ... not knowing what you are going to get means you've got something to look forward to, so immediately you are interested and excited about what's coming up.
143	if you've had a really rubbish week... you get an atmosphere. Particularly with the pub—it's full of really interested, enthusiastic people, so you pick up on that vibe and the emotions that everybody else has. So, you get excited and interested, so

FIGURE 5.3

As another option to gather quotes, here are the same concepts from the transcript grouped together and tagged with an identification number so this speaker's name remains private. Colors are optional here.

> If you are pulling quotes out and putting them in a document or
> spreadsheet, you'll want to tag the quote with the speaker who
> said it. This way, if you don't understand the context of a quote,
> you can go back to the source transcript. To preserve privacy and
> prevent demographic preconceptions from influencing you later,
> try using an identification number instead of the speaker's name.

Sometimes you can't do the review until days after the listening session. That's not a problem; you can do the review as much as a year
later. It doesn't matter, as long as the listening session was conducted
reasonably well and the transcript (or written conversation) is clear
and includes some indication of the emotional tone of the speaker
(or writer), for example, sarcasm.

Make Sense of Each Concept

What you are essentially doing with the transcript is taking out all
the superfluous words. This exercise helps you discover the different
kernels of what the speaker meant to convey. It's a tiny bit similar to
what the author and poet Austin Kleon does. He takes a newspaper
story and blacks out all the words except those that he feels are
vital, and he makes a poem out of them. You're doing something
similar with the quotes. You're blacking out all the extra words (see
Figure 5.4), as the speaker tried to explain his thoughts, until you get
down to the true meaning of each concept he was trying to express.

How granular should each discrete concept be? You want each
one to represent a single guiding principle, a single reaction, or a
single part of the thinking process. Make each concept, whether it's
made up of one quote or strung together from several places in the
transcript, represent a unique idea. It could be that the speaker is
talking about an idea, but that idea is spread across many paragraphs
in the transcript. It's just one idea. As the story continues, it wan-
ders. The speaker is thinking aloud, and sometimes changes topics
mid-sentence when he thinks of something related. Or he may even
change his mind mid-sentence. Collect all the little bits into one pile.
Or just collect one or two representative quotes and ignore the rest
of the repeats.

FIGURE 5.4
One of Austin Kleon's
newspaper blackout
poems from his blog
at austinkleon.com,
September 2, 2013.
(Reprinted with
permission.)

Here's where you can measure how well you are doing in the listening sessions. When you listen to someone telling a story, you fill
in a lot of details that go unsaid. These "fillers" are based on your
cultural and personal history—and probably half the time they're
wrong. In the listening session, it's hard to notice these places where
you've filled in your own meaning. Simple things are usually the
culprits. Someone says, "I hold weekly team meetings," and you
think you know what's going on. Instead, you're filling in meaning
based on your own experiences of weekly meetings. Try to notice
these fillers in the transcript and, in your next listening session, prod
yourself to ask the speaker his reasoning. "Why the meetings?"

What to Skip in the Transcript

You're not going to be using every word from the transcript. There
is some stuff that gets said by way of setting a scene, or as a way
of figuring out how to explain something, that you can skip. There
might even be whole swaths of the conversation where the speaker
was generalizing or citing opinions that you can go past, so you can

get to the deeper part that helps develop your empathy. There will be quotes that look tantalizingly meaningful, but when you grab them, their relevance melts away. Instead of tearing your hair out trying to conceptualize their significance, you can largely ignore certain things. None of these items in the following list directly helps you develop empathy. It's what lies beneath these things that you want to move on to.

- Explanation of event, process, or scene
- Statement of fact
- Opinion
- Preference
- Generalization
- Passive behavior
- Conjecture
- Concepts that are out of scope

Explanation of Event, Process, or Scene

Descriptions of what was happening, where someone was, and how something works tend to come at the beginning of a story—although not always. These descriptions are necessary. A speaker can't leave them out, or you won't understand what is going on. But neither the scene nor the process being explained will help you develop empathy. You can skip over these parts of the transcript. Of course, sometimes a bit of the scene-setting is useful to add to the collection of quotes for a concept, just for context, to help you understand the concept a few months from now.

Statement of Fact

Sometimes a speaker wants you to know certain facts. He might mention, for example, what he owns, how he gets to work, who he knows, where an event took place, or when he started working somewhere. Notice these examples include those five words you were taught at school to include in your writing: *who, what, when, where,* and *how*. It turns out these little facts serve as *background to the action*. Background facts, by themselves, do not help you develop empathy. Like explanations, they help the speaker set a scene for subsequent descriptions of reasoning, decision-making, and reactions.

So, when you are studying the transcript, you can skip the background facts and get straight to the deep stuff. The deep stuff represents the *why*. That's the sixth word that goes with the *who-what-when* litany.

Opinion

Opinions are the thin crust[1] over a person's deeper reasoning and guiding principles (see Figure 5.5). An opinion represents a view about a particular thing or condition that is based on a person's guiding principle. Opinions are intrinsically tied to the context they are about. Guiding principles, by comparison, are not tied to one particular instance. For example, a speaker could say he thinks no one in drought-prone areas should have living grass lawns because they require so much irrigation. If you ask how he formed his opinion, you might hear statements of fact about how much water is needed to keep a lawn green, and then you'd eventually divine a guiding principle like, "natural resources are not infinite and therefore should not be wasted." His guiding principle could apply to many situations: water, coal, oil.

Opinions often try to masquerade as emotional reactions or guiding principles. A person might use the English phrases "feel that" or "feel like." These phrases trick you into thinking they herald emotions, because of the word "feel," but they actually introduce opinions. Likewise, the English phrase "I believe" tricks you into thinking it reveals a belief, but it more frequently announces an opinion. There might be similar misdirecting phrases in other languages, so be on the lookout for them.

Incidentally, in cultures where people are shy about giving opinions, you'll notice that the empathetic style of listening—where you never ask for an opinion—works wonderfully. A person from such a culture will feel much more comfortable in a conversation where opinion and preference never come up (see Figure 5.5).

You will run across places in a transcript where you did not recognize an opinion and did not dig into the background of why it had formed. It's impossible to catch them all in the moment. Or maybe the opinion seemed unimportant at the time. Abstain from guessing about what principle is behind the opinion. Maybe you can go back to the speaker and ask about his reasoning, but if you can't, you have to ignore that part of the transcript.

---

1 See also Mark Twain's autobiography, *Early Fragments*, as he speaks about writing an autobiography. "All day long, and every day, the mill of his brain is grinding, and his thoughts … are his history. His acts and his words are merely the visible, thin crust of his world."

FIGURE 5.5

Opinions are the thin crust over a person's deeper reasoning and guiding principles.

When you are developing empathy with customers, you or your team might be questioned about why you're skipping over opinions. If this is the case, explain how the randomness of opinions, and the shades and nuances involved, usually result in no patterns across different people.

Preference

Like opinions, preferences are representations of deeper reasoning and behavior. If someone mentions a preference, you'll want to keep reading the transcript to find out why that preference was developed. The reason might appear a few paragraphs later. Understanding the reasoning beneath a preference is what will help you develop empathy with this person.

There are some tricky words used with preferences where you can't tell whether you should skip them or not. The words "hate," "love," and "like" might indicate an emotional reaction instead of a preference. Keep reading for context. Perhaps someone says, "I hate business trips," and a few sentences on you find out he gets anxious and has had small panic attacks while flying. So you can skip the preference about business trips and focus on his emotional terror of flying and his reasoning about trying to cancel a particular business trip.

Furthermore, the word "hate" may come up as a complaint about something. "I hate it when …." Whether it's about your organization's offering or about something else entirely, keep reading to find out what the person *did* about the situation.

---

2 Interview with Nate Bolt, by Jay Cassano, FastCompany Labs, fastcolabs.com, "Secrets from Facebook's Mobile UX Testing Team," April 8, 2013.

Generalization

Unfortunately, lots of people have a habit of speaking in generalities. Instead of describing a particular instance or moment of time, they describe all similar moments as one—the average sorts of moment. During the listening session, you might have had limited success convincing a speaker to tell you stories specific to one place and time, even though you asked clearly and provided examples. Some people just have a strong habit of speaking in a broad, vague, reductive manner.

With this kind of speaker, you may have actually had to end the session early. Peer through the transcript and see if you can spot some reasoning, an emotion, or a guiding principle. There might be a few places where you got something descriptive of the speaker's thinking process. But, typically, with a transcript full of generalizations, you will only be able to collect a couple of quotes from it.

Passive Behavior

A passive behavior is when something happens to a person, not something a person does. Skip it because the speaker hasn't done any thinking or reacting yet. Read on until you come across his reaction to this thing that happened. "I read the email about the last-minute change that Sam made" may seem like an action—reading—but it's simply information being put into this speaker's mind. It's passive. It is the speaker's reaction that you are interested in: "So I stormed down to Sam's office and demanded an explanation. I was so angry at his lack of courtesy toward the team that had spent a week discussing what he had so blithely changed." This latter description gets deeper into the speaker's emotional reaction and reasoning.

Conjecture

When you ask someone to make guesses about future decisions or behavior, you are asking for conjecture. It's speculation about how the speaker will react or what he will do, and why. And because it hasn't happened yet, it doesn't count toward empathy. Even though it might contain reasoning, reactions, and guiding principles, it's all just a guess. Skip it.

People might fall into talking about their future actions simply because they are aware that journalists, marketing surveys, and usability researchers often ask these questions. Again, hopefully, you recognized the conjecture during the listening session and coaxed the speaker back to stories of what he actually experienced. Usually, the key word that indicates conjecture is "would," so it will be easy to spot in a transcript.

Concepts That Are Out of Scope

When you study the transcript, you have the advantage of knowing how pieces of the speaker's story relate and how they compare with what other speakers said. You are better able to decide if a particular part matters to you or not. If several other people in other transcripts also talk about similar things, then it's not actually out of scope. If it's somewhat tied in to the emotional content of what was said, it is, likewise, in scope. Include these pieces in your quotes.

What's "scope," exactly? It is the subject of interest that you explored with the speaker. With someone who is a direct report to you in your organization, the scope might be the project he's working on for you or the skills he's improving. With a customer of an enterprise software suite, the scope might be how he decides which software to pursue and maintain, or how he keeps track of all the employees at his multinational organization. So, if part of the transcript dwells on the surprise of meeting coworkers at the day-care facility across town where he drops his kids off, that's out of scope. But a decision to look up some work information because of a comment that a coworker made, no matter if it happened at the day-care facility or not, is in scope.

Your Goal Is to Get Better

Studying the transcript will also help you get better at the listening sessions—better at getting those rich descriptions into the transcript. You'll be better able to recognize the three things that build empathy as people are saying them: reasoning, reactions, and guiding principles. You'll also be able to see the places where you should have asked the speaker for more detail, instead of staying at the superficial level of statement of fact or opinion. A review helps you learn how to listen. This extension of your listening practice allows you to improve within weeks or months, instead of taking months or years.

Write a Summary of Each Concept

Now that you have a collection of quotes that represent non-repeating, discrete concepts, there is an additional step you can take. You can write a summary of each discrete concept. This exercise is optional, but it is *powerful*. Writing or crafting words engages a part of your brain that creates meaning and sense. It helps your mind reach an even deeper understanding.

Writing summaries serves three purposes:

- It provides you with a set of written artifacts representing your knowledge, which you can use in many parts of your work.

- It helps further clarify the ambiguity of what a person said. When you look at a quote representing a roundabout way of getting to a concept, it takes a few seconds to comprehend the meaning. If you can summarize that quote more clearly, then when you read it a month from now, you'll understand it immediately.

- Systematize quotes across different people so you can compare them later. Done correctly, making summaries conform to a certain format will allow you to make comparisons and find patterns more quickly.

The written summaries can be used in several ways. You can consult the summaries before the next listening session with the same person, to remind yourself of previous concepts, and after the listening session, you can look at the summaries to gauge changes. You can track skills and development in the people you manage. You can observe what is of concern to your leaders over time.

For the process of creation, you can use memorable summaries in presentations and to disseminate awareness around your organization. You can employ memorable summaries as inspiration or proof in creative sessions. You can put all the summaries in lists, group them, or stack them. Summaries can appear in maps and diagrams and scenarios. You can compare groups of summaries and use them in strategic discussions. The summaries are evergreen, which means they are timeless. Because summaries have no reference to tools or processes, you can apply them again and again over decades of working with the type of person you developed empathy with.

If you can afford to, write the summaries together with your team. Summarizing together as a group allows your team to come to agreement about the meaning, and later use that solidified agreement as a strength in design discussions. You can certainly write summaries solo, as the team is not crucial to the process. But in large organizations, forging a group understanding has benefits that sometimes outweigh the additional time-cost of having multiple people working on the same thing.

> **NOTE** WHICH SUMMARIES AND WHEN?
>
> If you prefer, you can write the summary as soon as you collect the quotes together, instead of collecting all the quotes first. Or you can go in fits and spurts. Or, possibly, pick some of the quotes that are more important to your organization and just summarize those. Do it in any way that feels achievable to you.

Start with the Verb

Your first step in writing a summary is to come up with a verb that represents the intent of what the person was thinking, deciding, or feeling. Jot down the first verb that comes to mind. Next, think of a second verb, just in case the first one is not perfectly clear. See if you can think of a third verb and a fourth one. The more verbs you think of, the closer you'll come to the most unambiguous, expressive verb that you should choose. If one of the stronger verbs you think of happens to be a verb the speaker used, then choose that one, because it will help you remember how he said it.

As an aid, you may also want to jot down the type of summary you're trying to write: thinking and reasoning, reaction, or guiding principle.

If it seems difficult to think of a good verb, maybe you are thinking about the wrong part of the concept. Find the key part of what is being explained. You may have to break down the words of the quote to get at it; you may have to dissect the language being used. Read between the lines to get the context, intonation, and connotation of the sentences that were uttered. It's more than the meaning of each word—it's word association and invoking imagery. It's the cultural background, popular references, and the social norms of what should not be said directly. It's sarcasm, being flip, or cynical, or self-deprecating. It's what the laughter means in different contexts: amusement, pain, irony, self-deprecation, the-system-is-against-us, and so on. To solve the linguistic puzzles represented by the quotes, you almost have to ignore the words themselves to figure out what the person was trying to communicate.

Another reason that picking a verb may be difficult is because the quote is not yet complete—there might be another sentence this person says later that belongs to this concept. The later quote may contain that illustrative verb. Set the summary aside for a while, on the chance that you will encounter the other part of the puzzle a little later.

Why a Verb?

Why start with a verb? First, you want an easy way to compare this summary to past summaries or to all the other summaries from other speakers. If you use the same verb-first format for all summaries, it will be much easier to compare.

Moreover, verbs are closer to the action than nouns. You can imagine the experience of a verb. Nouns represent objects, or maybe categories, or aspects. Nouns can bring a few unconscious assumptions with them. For example, what assumption do you make when you hear, "I needed time for *relaxation*?" Consequently, verbs make much better candidates for summarizing the things that help you develop empathy.

Unfortunately, you're up against some ingrained practices. Research and reports traditionally focus on nouns. You might have to fight your organization's tendency to classify things into predefined, noun-labeled boxes. So in this way, using verbs might help you reframe things. Verbs will help you and your coworkers more easily see new perspectives.

Another habit to fight is making your verbs into gerunds. Gerunds are verbs with "ing" added to them: wondering, yelling, feeling. Adding "ing" makes a verb into a noun—a noun that can be boxed up and kept at a distance, rather than experienced as an action.

First Person, Present Tense

Imagine the personal pronoun "I" when you create your summary verb. Even though the transcript may contain third-person verbs—because in English people often talk about themselves in the third person while storytelling—twist it around to the first person. If you use third person, you have created a sentence where the actor is someone other than yourself. The goal of developing empathy with a person is to be able to "walk in his shoes." If you keep referring to his reasoning in third person, *you* never step into his shoes. For example, "*He* yelled at the coach because he was not paying attention when it happened" is about another person yelling, not about you yelling. It's easier to feel judgmental or misinterpret a perspective. If you use first person in the present tense, suddenly you're there in his shoes. *"I yell at the coach because he was not paying attention when it happened."* There is a magical difference.

Additionally, you may be reading your summaries two months or two years from now. For consistency, you want to represent the experience as current, something that is going through someone's mind in the present.

Being "present," acting out someone else's story, is the gateway to empathy.

Convey Emotional Reactions as Verbs

Use the verb "feel" to represent emotional reactions and follow it immediately with a word representing the emotion being felt. "Feel" + emotion. Use this equation for most emotions, except the few emotions that have their own verb form, at least in English (see Figure 5.6). If you get stuck trying to find the perfect word to describe the emotion, try using a thesaurus, or there's a "feelings-inventory" list on the Center for Nonviolent Communication website.[3]

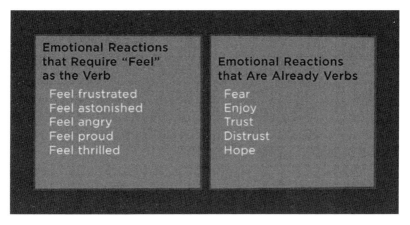

FIGURE 5.6
Usually, you will use the verb "feel" to represent emotional reactions. There are some exceptions in English, which are perfectly good to use as verbs.

---

3 At publication, the list of emotions is at www.cnvc.org/training/feelings-inventory.

Watch out for the English word "feeling." If you asked the speaker about how he "feels," you might see a response that describes not an emotional state but a physical state. Just because the word "feel" is in the transcript doesn't automatically mean it's an emotion (see Figure 5.7).

FIGURE 5.7
In English, someone might use the word "feel" to describe a physical sensation, not an emotion. Skip these.

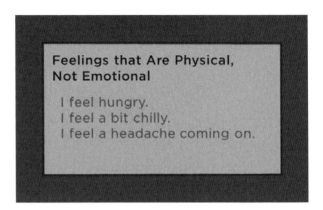

Feelings that Are Physical, Not Emotional

I feel hungry.
I feel a bit chilly.
I feel a headache coming on.

As mentioned earlier, the word "feel" creeps into use when a speaker is voicing an opinion or conjecture. In English, people will say, "I feel that ..." or "I feel like ..." to announce an opinion or a desire. One way to be aware of these examples is to recognize when the word just after "feel" is not an emotion. "That" and "like" are not emotions. So, when you see the word "feel" in the transcript, don't assume it's an emotion being described. Keep reading, and perhaps you'll see some deeper exploration later that you can use.[4]

When you see the verb "wish," it's about a future state or an alternate scenario to a past experience; it's conjecture. Skip it. But when you see the verb "hope," you can interpret that as an emotion. It's the emotion a person has right now about something that might happen in the future. It's not conjecture about an emotion in the future, nor even conjecture about the event in the future. It's an emotion the person is feeling now.

There is another tricky emotional verb. Watch out for the English expression "I hate myself when ...." Usually "hate" is a preference that you can skip. However, in this case, it's an emotion a person is direct-ing at himself. He is annoyed or angry at himself for something. For

---

4 Some of these problems may not be issues in other languages.

clarity's sake, go ahead and use the alternate emotional vocabulary in your summary. However, if the phrase "hate myself" really helps you remember this particular story, then use "hate" as your summary verb.

The goal is to be able to clearly become the person in your mind when you read the summary later. Writing these summaries is a part of developing the empathy that you can later invoke.

Verbs to Avoid

There are a few verbs that don't lend any clarity to a summary (see Figure 5.8). When you read unclear verbs later, you find yourself obliged to reread all the quotes just to understand that person again. Save yourself that time and choose a sparkling verb instead.

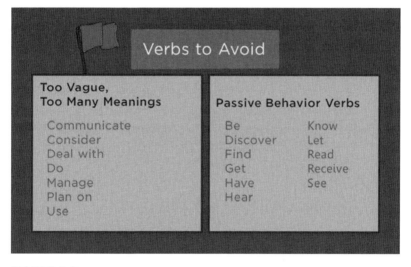

FIGURE 5.8
Verbs that are unclear or not active are hard to understand later.
Avoid these verbs.

There are probably other English verbs that should be on the "Verbs to Avoid" list. With every transcript you read, exercise your judgment. For example, the verb "miss" can be passive: "The ball barely missed my head." Or it can be used as a statement of fact: "I missed the train yet again this morning." Or it can be used as an emotion: "I miss my summer holidays when …." Only in the last instance is it valid for developing empathy, and you could summarize more clearly with "I feel nostalgic for my summer holidays when …." Any time you grapple with a verb that doesn't seem quite clear enough, consider changing it to something a bit more evocative.

Write the Rest of the Summary

Now that you have a verb to start your summary, complete the sentence. Keep it to one sentence. The brevity will make it faster to read later.

Summaries need to be succinct and relate the core of what the speaker intended. Summaries also need to speak to the context. So clarify your summary by putting the reason for the behavior right after the verb.

> **NOTE** AVOID CRYSTALLIZING, DISTILLING, OR SYNTHESIZING
>
> Avoid crystallizing or distilling a larger meaning from a collection of quotes that represent a concept. Simply restate, more clearly, what this *one* speaker was trying to communicate to you. Don't try to show what this quote signifies in a broader sense, across different people. Save the generalization and synthesis until later; right now, you are still in the stage of developing empathy.

Edit Until It's Clean and Clear

Because you're going to use the summary for various purposes, focus on brevity. Part of the idea of writing a summary is to create a faster way to understand the quotes you collected, without having to read through the details and make sense of them again months later. You want the summary to be clean and not confusing. You want to be able to say it aloud and have it flow nicely off your tongue.

Think of your sentence like a mobile. The verb that is the top, with the object just below it, and a few phrases hanging, balanced, off of that.[5] If your sentence is a mobile, don't build it with extra parts that either don't hang together, are impossible to say aloud, or are actually two sentences glued together awkwardly, causing the mobile to tip to one side (see Figure 5.9).

---

5 Good sentence-diagramming tools and links, http://compsocsci.blogspot.com/ 2011/11/resources-on-nlp-sentence-diagramming.html.

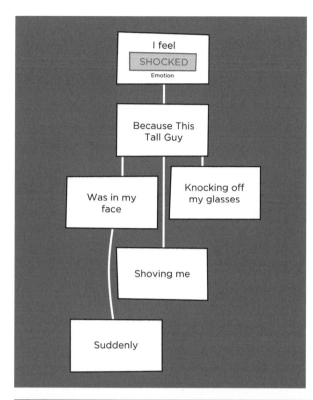

FIGURE 5.9
To the left is a good, clean summary sentence, diagrammed as a balanced mobile. Below is a summary that is a jumble of clauses and does not hang together.

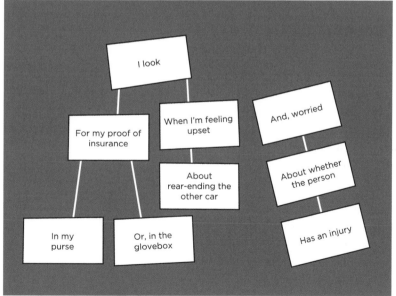

Try to evoke the feel of the quote, but don't force it. Every detail doesn't have to show up—just details that will help you remember this person's story. You can use some of the person's own phrasing to remind yourself of the story. This shouldn't be an overwhelming exercise. You don't have to flail around forcing together a collage of phrases or write a summary that is just as long as the quote. There is no one perfect way to get the summary "right." If you spend too much time trying to craft a summary, you're overdoing it.

Ensure That Each Summary Is a Unique Thought

Each concept should only show up once for that speaker. He may refer to the same idea over and over in the transcript, describing it a little better each time, but you should have gathered those distinct quotes together. Only one summary represents the entire set of quotes regarding that one concept.

Likewise, avoid using the same quote in two different summaries. The quote ought to be in service of one unique concept. Even if the quote can be interpreted to be supporting two different concepts, choose one. Keep it simple.

Avoid Compound Sentences

A compound sentence is two sentences glued together with a conjunction (*and, but, so, yet, or, nor, for*).[6] Each sentence has its own actor and verb, and usually an object. "I serve the cake, but she does not want any." Do not write compound sentences as summaries. As a way to check this, look for the word "and" in your summaries. Even if it's a simple sentence, with only one actor but with two verbs, rewrite it. You probably have two separate ideas. "I decide to leave the meeting early *and start* doing other things that make better use of my time." If this is true, divide them (and the relevant quotes) into two summaries. "I decide to leave the meeting" is separate from "I make better use of my time by starting to do other things."

Sometimes the ideas are so related, however, that it's better to join them together using a phrase starting with *because, even though, despite, although, since, whereas*, etc. "I decide to leave the meeting early *because* I have better things to do." The important point that you want

---

6 By contrast, a complex sentence is a sentence that has a bunch of phrases (called dependent clauses) in addition to the main part of the sentence where you see the actors, the verb, and the object.

to summarize is the decision to leave the meeting; the "better things to do" is the speaker's reasoning in support of his decision.

Conjunctions themselves are not the culprits. You can use "and" to join two descriptions together. "I feel elated by the praise and support of my boss, who usually does not talk to me." Just don't join two verbs together. "I *feel elated but laugh* to myself about the praise from my boss, because he usually does not talk to me." These are two separate concepts, each deserving its own separate summary.

Write a summary that would make your grammar teacher proud. Follow the rules of syntax. Add decent punctuation. You want to aim for a single, complex sentence that is easily readable.

Carry Along the Quotes

When writing summaries with any digital tool, you can carry along the quotes, for easy reference later on (see Figure 5.10). This method is data rich but not required—an understanding of what each pile represents is all that is necessary. Handwritten notes are just as good.

Summary	ID	Quote
Feel impressed that the musicians do their thing to play a jam session with whoever decides to show up that day	143	a jam s take tur You jus along a get, bed Each pe perform They ar And, I r
Feel pleased that my small, friendly, non-chain pub makes made me feel so comfortable	143	Usually local pu So, it's feeling … it's ni
Relax with a drink and companionship	143	I can ha a relaxa meet uj just rela
Celebrate the start of our weekend with the ritual of going to the pub Friday night	143	I meet weeker … Two
Make sure I don't burn out from the stress of work	143	I work I … tense
Feel pleased that our pub attracts good musicians, from all over the UK	143	really g bands f stuff.

FIGURE 5.10

These are the same quotes that appeared earlier in this chapter, with summaries written for each concept.

Read It Aloud

If you're forging these summaries solo, you'll be amazed how easy it is to spot clarity problems when you read the summaries aloud. There is a book that explains how intonation and rhythm[7] help you articulate an idea, and how reading your work aloud really helps you with revisions.

Also, if you are doing this exercise solo, but you will be using the summaries to spread knowledge throughout your organization, it really makes sense to double-check what you've written with someone who might be able to point out where you are making assumptions.

Ideally, you would go back to the speaker and ask him to verify your summaries. In the book about interviewing customers, *InterViews*, the authors discuss whether it is acceptable to work with your own understanding of the transcript, or to go back to the participant and give him a chance to change the way you've summarized things.[8] This extra step may lead to more time spent circling around someone's concept of themselves, but if you have the time and resources to involve the participants in a review of your summaries, it has the potential to correct a few nuances.

Summary

The two advantages of studying the transcript—doubling your understanding of a person, and learning how to listen better—are really worth your time. Making sense of what a person said from the transcript provides double the depth of understanding than just simply listening does. The summaries are timeless and will continue to be useful for years. Yet, if you need to hurry toward a specific deadline, summaries are optional.

---

7 David Elbow, Professor of English Emeritus and the former Director of the Writing Program at the University of Massachusetts Amherst, *Vernacular Eloquence*, Chapter 5, "Intonation," and Chapter 11, "Revising by Reading Aloud." New York: Oxford University Press, 2012.

8 Kvale, Steinar, and Svend Brinkmann, *InterViews*, Chapter 4, "Ethical Issues of Interviewing," 2nd ed., page 63. Thousand Oaks: SAGE Publications, 2008.

PICK OUT THE CONCEPTS

- Make sense of how the concepts come together.
- What to skip in the transcript:
    - Explanation of event, process, or scene
    - Statement of fact
    - Opinion
    - Preference
    - Generalization
    - Passive behavior
    - Conjecture
    - Concepts that are out of scope

WRITE A SUMMARY OF EACH CONCEPT

- Start with a verb.
- Write the rest of the summary.
- Edit until it's clean and clear:
    - Ensure that each summary is a unique thought.
    - Avoid compound sentences.
    - Read it aloud.

Cultivate the soil
within your organization so
empathy can take root and grow.

Apply Empathy to What You Create

In this chapter, the focus is on using empathy—in particular, for the things you create in your work. Empathy allows you to expand the number of angles you consider when you make something—it increases your horizon. Because you have multiplied your understanding of the purposes people are trying to achieve, you now have a better sense of where you want to shift and adjust how you support those purposes. For example, instead of leaping to the conclusion that people need a faster way to file their purchase orders or take attendance in a class, you might instead help people skip these tedious tasks and focus on activities that require uniquely human engagement. You can explore better ways to support the intent, customized for certain types of behavior.

Empathy is not always about revelation. Often, the knowledge developed from empathy is not surprising: it consists of stuff you already know, but possibly didn't pay a lot of attention to or maybe misremembered. Even if it does seem obvious in retrospect, the reminder is powerful enough to have it documented.

Empathy will also improve your clarity about your strategy. You will be able to deliberate with intelligence between options in terms of target audience or direction. You'll be able to plan beyond the minimally viable product. And, if you're curious, you will be able to pinpoint where believable guesses in the past led your organization astray.

NOTE THE THINGS YOU MAKE

The phrase "things you make" encompasses a broad range. These things can be physical or digital. Moreover, they can be internal to your organization or external—facing partners, customers, vendors, or others. They can be significant things that take months to craft or tiny things that only take 15 minutes to make. Some of these things are not traditionally thought of as requiring empathy to create.

- Product
- Process
- Content
- Service
- Policy

Anything that enables others to understand or achieve something comes under this heading. To this point, the phrase "your work" doesn't just refer to activities you get paid for. It can also mean volunteer activities or any role you regularly take on for a group of people: coach, planner, advisor, etc.

Empathy is often used for persuasion. Instead, for the highest impact on your work, use empathy in support of people. Empathy in support means being willing to acknowledge another person's intent and work with it, morphing your own intent because of the empathy you developed. This is the empathic mindset.

Look for Patterns

In the previous chapters of this book, you practiced emptying your mind so you could absorb and understand someone else's thinking and reactions. Beginning with this chapter, you will start applying the knowledge you gathered. You get to unleash your powers of analysis and pattern recognition to synthesize some larger observations from the things people told you.

This work potentially involves editing summaries, if you have them, to clarify any uncertainties. It's about splitting up summaries that got accidentally jammed together. Then it's about figuring out what the *intent* was behind the thinking and using that intent to gather together similar summaries from other people. And, it's also about deciding what to leave out for now.

If you don't have summaries, you can do all this in a more intuitive manner. Mentally and verbally, you review similarities you see across different people, and then you jot down what the overall intent was for each trend you recognize. Because these patterns are written in broad terms, a good portion of all the concepts detailed using summaries will actually be covered—around 25%–30%. That's good enough for a lot of circumstances.

Cognitively, you are using a different process in your mind than when you were developing empathy. For the summaries, you were strictly summarizing what you thought each person was trying to express. For the patterns across the stories, you will be using your analytic mind to find similarities (see Figure 6.1). Usually, people are better at one or the other—summarizing or analyzing. If you're lucky, and you work on a team, you have a balance of skills so that team members can do different parts of the work. And if you don't have a balance—or if you are a solo practitioner—that's why the summaries are optional and from-memory pattern-finding is viable.

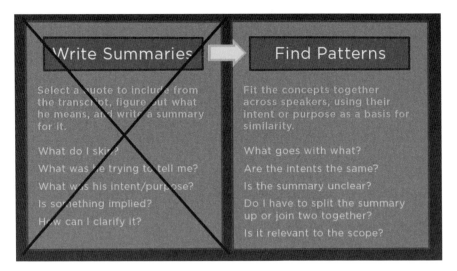

FIGURE 6.1

Now you can aggregate concepts across different people. You will also double-check that the information is presented clearly and is relevant to your scope.

Quick Method: Seek Patterns by Memory

If you did not write summaries, you'll seek patterns in what you remember that people said. This is a faster method, so it comes with some drawbacks. The main drawback is your memory and the tricks it plays with the significance, frequency, and meaning behind what people said. With this method, it's probably better to stick to the really obvious concepts that people brought up and skip the little details that you might not have remembered correctly.

As you hear each additional story, you might start noticing patterns. You can make note of these patterns after each listening session, but don't forget to amend your notes when it turns out a "pattern" was only between two people. You'll want to pay attention to the bigger patterns—those that stretch across more people.

You might have transcripts of each session, so that's an additional way to remind yourself of what people were saying. Take a bit of time to review your post-session notes or those transcripts before you start to summarize the bigger patterns.

A good collaborative way to do this is, after a listening session, for team members to record the outstanding concepts for that person in a shared spreadsheet. Team members can also spend a little time putting the concepts in some sort of order. After the next session, new lines are added to the spreadsheet next to earlier related concepts. You can mark each line with an identification number in case you want to track down the source later. Note that this work takes place after each session so that the full attention of every listener is on the person during the session.

Rich Method: Look for Patterns Across Summaries

If you have summaries and want to get all the details corralled in your patterns, the most important point to know is that this process of finding patterns cannot be automated. You can't put all the same verbs together or all the "feel relieved" reactions together. Each summary *means* a different thing, and most of those meanings are nuanced. To find the patterns, consider each one of them separately. It may sound overwhelming, but it is absorbing work and goes fast, especially for minds that fall into flow with this kind of work.

Estimate the Hours Needed

To find all the patterns, you will need about 20 hours for a set of 300 summaries. That means going through 15 summaries an hour. You may not use absolutely all the summaries—only the concepts that feel like relevant patterns—so this number could turn out to be lower.

You *can* make this happen within a work week, if you happen to have a couple other people to work with. Do half of the work together as a group, in little intervals, and the other half of the work individually.

For example, schedule a two-hour working session with your team once a day. That's 10 hours. Then assign a team member to work on the patterns solo for two hours each day, where it rotates, so that everybody can get their *other* work done, too. For example, Alix owns it for two hours Monday and Wednesday. Barrie owns it for two hours Tuesday and Friday. Camille owns it for two hours Thursday. This makes up the other 10 hours of effort.

Consider One Summary at a Time

It's easiest to start with one summary, find other summaries that seem similar in concept, and then move on to another.[1] After several passes through the whole set of data, the only summaries left will be those you're not interested in. This technique is known as *affinity grouping*.

Pick one summary that interests you. It doesn't really matter which one, but choose a concept that you remember other people also talking about. As you find similar summaries from other people, place them next to the first summary. This physical "placing" can happen in a text document, a spreadsheet, with sticky notes, index cards, or however else you like to work.

The first pass through your summaries will take longer than any subsequent pass. To get started faster, have several people working on it at the same time, connected remotely or in the same room. Divide up all the summaries so that each person "owns" a different subset to scan through. As you pair concepts, discuss aloud the underlying intent that binds them together. As a team, you can get through 10–15 summaries in the course of an hour.

> **TIP** USE THE VERB AS SHORTHAND
>
> When you are working together and want to use a single word as shorthand to refer to a summary, say the verb that begins the summary. Or say a few of the verbs of the summaries that are collected in a group. "Does this new summary belong with the 'wonder-consider' set or the 'decide-choose-select' set?" Verbs are more illustrative than nouns for describing behavior. (Also, this is a good test to see if your verbs are vague or expressive.)

Momentum is important, especially in the face of everyday demands on your time at work. You will probably want to get this done quickly. The advantage of being quick is that your memory of the other patterns will remain fresh. Drawing it out over months means that you're reacquainting yourself with existing patterns again and again. Choose the approach that works best for the moment and stay flexible, changing your approach for subsequent rounds; different circumstances may arise that require a different pace. It all depends on how you want to work at each juncture.

---

1 This is also the first step toward creating the top half of a mental model diagram— where the second step is to make hierarchies out of the affinity groups you create. In the case of simply developing empathy, you do not need to take the second step.

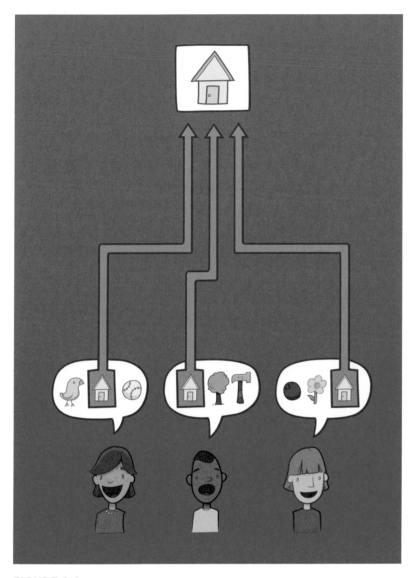

FIGURE 6.2
Finding patterns is about looking for a concept with the same underlying purpose across individuals.

What do the patterns end up looking like when everyone you listened to has been studied, summarized, and aggregated? You will find some concepts that four or five or more "voices" bring up (see Figure 6.2). You will find other concepts represented by only two or three voices. In the example from an insurance company that studied near-miss accidents (see Figure 6.3), four different voices said they "wondered what the other person involved was thinking," while only two voices said they "imagined that the person who did this wasn't paying attention." The number of voices does not indicate the importance of a pattern; importance is determined by your organization's current focus. Also, you don't have to formally label the patterns this way, although it helps to have something to call them.

Wonder what the other person involved was thinking	
Attempt to see things from his point of view, as someone who does not do flip turns	101
Wonder what drives the kind of anger that causes a person to strike out violently at a stranger	102
Try to think what was going through the young man's mind at the time	117
Realize based on her story, the guard was paying attention but made an assumption	101
Assume the guy who jumped in the deep end could swim, because an adult would be smarter than that	123
Imagine how the person who did this wasn't paying attention	
Feel frustrated that the driver and occupants of the work vehicle appear to have no idea the damage they caused me	117
Imagine the young guy was not paying attention because he was listening to music as he drove his truck fast	117
Feel angry replaying the scenario from his eyes and seeing myself in the middle of the lane on my back, clearly unaware of him	101
Think about what would have happened if	
Imagine that if he was armed, he would have shot or stabbed me	102
Imagine what would have happened if I had been 10 steps behind	109
Imagine what would have happened if I had turned into the crosswalk immediately or been five steps ahead of myself	117
Imagine what would have happened if the truck driver hadn't been paying attention	123
Imagine how horrible it would have been if he'd drowned while I was watching	123
Feel chilled how close my son had been from having a reaction to the peanut butter	105
Feel terrified when I imagine that freeway driver not paying attention for a second or two, and causing an injury accident	110
Try not to drive myself crazy thinking of scary scenarios like these where I have no control over damage or injury	117

FIGURE 6.3

An insurance company explored how people "experience a near-miss accident," and these are three (of 32) aggregated patterns of thinking. The numbers in the column to the right of each summary represent each person's unique ID number, in case you want to trace back to the quote and the transcript to reassess or explain the context.

You can list the patterns in roughly chronological order, although the order is not important—it just helps your team find a pattern in the list more easily. You can put the few patterns that are outside of the chronology (the overarching patterns that happen contiguously) at the end of the list.

You'll know you're all finished when everything left is unique to different people. Some of these leftovers are generalizations, which shouldn't have been made into summaries. These generalizations can be deleted. Several of these leftover ideas might be interesting to your organization, but you need to hear more evidence from other people.

Wrap Your Mind Around the Difficult Ones

Sometimes you find a pattern that ends up being just one person's voice, restating the same thing over and over. It isn't a pattern, because it's only one person. No one else said anything similar. You have a choice. You can ignore these statements entirely, or if they seem to be of importance to your organization, you can find new people and conduct additional listening sessions to see if the topic comes up again. Suggesting a change to your offerings based on one voice isn't logical, although it is tempting if the topic seems universal. Wait until you find come corroboration from other voices.

TIP ADDITIONAL LISTENING SESSIONS

If you do conduct additional listening sessions to see if there is corroboration out there for a concept only one person mentioned, be careful not to bring up that concept. You are never supposed to introduce topics to listening sessions because it might skew the results. If you do that, people will talk about your topic, even if they would have never brought it up on their own.

On the other hand, if it seems too difficult to make a match between two summaries, then maybe one summary isn't written quite right. Try editing the summary to see if you can bring out some clarity in the similarity. Alternatively, your edit might make the two summaries more distinct from each other. Clarify the summary with a better verb, or recast it as a reaction instead of thinking, or vice-versa.

Or possibly you will encounter two summaries from the same person about the same incident. Just delete one of them. You don't need to rigorously collect every instance of the concept from that one person.

If you don't want to delete one, then choose one summary and merge the quotes together. If the summaries are from the same person and describe the same concept but are from two different incidents, then go ahead and leave them both present if you like.

Assess Your Confidence

When you find patterns across listening sessions, how confident can you be about whether you got them right? Are they reliable? The degree to which the same concept repeats across different people is a good indicator of reliability in qualitative data.[2] If only one person talks about a concept, it is not a pattern. That is simple. If two people talk about a concept, it's a possible pattern—you judge whether to keep the concept by whether it is likely that others would also bring it up if you conducted more listening sessions. That is a judgment based on your own experience, so double-check it with as many peers in different areas as you can. If five people talk about a concept that seems foreign to you, it is a valid pattern despite your unfamiliarity. In the end, you will keep the concepts that are important to your organization, so the selection process should lean toward where you want to focus. Double-check this also, because a concept you leave behind might be more significant than you are used to thinking.

Finding patterns is an inductive process, not deductive. You might be used to working in a deductive manner, since that approach is used for most problem solving. But finding patterns in people's reasoning is not problem solving. For inductive reasoning, you don't start with a hypothesis—instead, you let things form a structure by their own characteristics.

- **Deductive is top-down:** Form a hypothesis, gather and evaluate data, and confirm or reject the hypothesis, which may then support or revise a theory you had.

- **Inductive is bottom-up:** Define a scope to explore, gather information, form a hypothesis based on that information, and explore the probable exceptions to this conclusion.[3] There is not epistemic[4] certainty.

---

2 Dr. Brené Brown, TEDxHouston, June 12, 2010, "The Power of Vulnerability" TED Talk.

3 See also "Introduction to Business Research Methods" by Anthony Yeong, July 10, 2011, slideshare.net

4 Epistemology means the study of knowledge.

There is also such a thing as false patterns. Humans have an innate talent for pattern recognition, but sometimes it can get carried away. A mild example is when you see a face in the components of a fire hydrant, a mailbox, or an electrical outlet, and suddenly these things are imbued with emotion, based on their "facial expressions." You feel sorry for the sad-looking mailbox. False patterns can occur when applying empathy, too. You might have something in mind, even subconsciously, and you mash different summaries together to represent this concept. You probably won't know you're creating a false pattern. The way to stop yourself is to quit when summaries get difficult to match. Difficulty could be the product of your mind's attempt to force summaries into a pattern you hope exists.

The Difference Between Summary- and Memory-Generated Patterns

The biggest advantage of memory-generated patterns is that they're quicker to pull together. If you have a small team, you may want to work this way most of the time. If your team needs the proof that summaries provide, so you can persuade others and make decisions with utmost confidence, then use memory-generated patterns only when there's a scope to explore that is already well understood.

The most obvious disadvantage of memory-generated patterns is that it relies on memory, and many concepts from the sessions will go missing.

The advantage of summary-generated patterns is that you don't miss anything that people said. You'll know how many voices mentioned a particular concept, and the concepts will be clarified and separated by nuances.

A disadvantage of summary-generated patterns is that, among all the detailed patterns, some of the concepts will seem less important to support from the point of view of the organization. Some of these patterns are just outside the organization's aim, so taking the time to list them might not be a good use of resources (see Figure 6.4).

	Advantage	Disadvantage
Memory-Generated	• Quick • Broad descriptions cover 25-30% of concepts • Covers high-value concepts the org is interested in	• Missing 70-75% of detailed concepts • Big ideas feel recurrent, but are not • Wording might be clouded by idiom of one person
Summary-Generated	• All concepts captured reliably • Easy to report contributors to pattern • Wording is clear • Nuances are evident • No doubting	• Some patterns are outside your focus • Can take a lot of time and discussion

FIGURE 6.4

Both approaches are valid for different circumstances. Pick the approach your situation demands, and be willing to switch your approach for subsequent rounds when needed.

Create Behavioral Segments from the Patterns

You've heard of marketing segments. They are defined groups of people in the market that your organization aims at. Marketing segments are just one kind of behavioral segment—where the behavior is "deciding to buy." There are myriad other kinds of behavioral segments, varying from industry to industry and between organizations within each industry. For example, in the airline industry, besides deciding to make a reservation, there are additional behaviors around contemplating a trip, deciding on flights, purchasing a ticket, and taking the flight itself. Segments help you organize your thinking around the people you support and the scenarios you are trying to help them through.

If you want to create representative groups of the people you support, the patterns you aggregated from the transcripts are a perfect source for discovering behavioral segments. You will find that some people you listened to have similar patterns of reasoning, and that there are nuanced distinctions between sets of people for a given situation. Each set of such people forms one behavioral segment. The type of behavior is defined by your scope of exploration. You name a set of segments by this behavior, such as "Deciding to Make Reservation Segments" and "Deciding on Flights Segments."

The summaries that make up the set of reasoning provide great character depth for the behavioral segment. Depth of character provides clarity and lends creativity to idea development.

As time goes on, you will conduct additional listening sessions and be faced with the question of how each additional person fits into existing behavioral segments. Most of the time, a new person fits into an existing segment easily. There is never an exact match, though. You want to look at the reasoning, reactions, and guiding principles of each segment and decide which set is closest, in general, to the new person. Sometimes, you'll encounter new people and realize there is yet another behavioral segment out there that you are just now discovering. Other times, you'll end up making changes to existing segments based on new patterns. There are also instances where the reasoning of one person changes based on phases, as in a person traveling to a business meeting versus going on a holiday. Don't think of your behavioral segments as rigidly defined groups; they're humans, and very few humans are that rigid in their behavior.

Behavioral Segments First, Then Maybe Personas

Each behavioral segment can be represented by a persona.[5] You do not have to represent a behavioral segment with a persona. You can work with the behavioral segments without turning them into individuals, with names, ages, faces, etc. But some people prefer the solidity of a persona as a reference point.

---

5 Personas are characters that represent different behavioral segments. See also Kim Goodwin's book *Designing for the Digital Age*. Indianapolis: Wiley, 2009.

If you do make personas, be careful. When you use them later, try not to let their demographics lead you astray from their behaviors. You might fall into the trap of thinking that the young age you assigned a persona, for example, dictates a different behavior than someone older. Maybe this young person likes to write movie reviews for her friends. It doesn't mean a 60-year-old doesn't also write movie reviews for the *New York Times*. They are both members of the same movie-review writing behavioral segment. To avoid this trap, try assigning the less common (at least in your mind) demographics to your persona. This trick will remind you to focus on the behavior of the segment, not the demographics. If you think of movie-review writers as young teenage reclusive boys, then make the persona an older, affable woman with lots of expertise and a humorous writing technique.

It's a Rotating Cast

A common misconception about these kinds of groups is that there is only one set of segments for your organization. Under this misconception, typically the segments represent the different "deciding to buy" behaviors. Instead of arguing with the group who created these marketing segments, think of it like an episodic television show with a large cast of characters. There are some characters that you use in certain scenes, and other characters that only make a few appearances. Each scene represents a different experience or touchpoint on a customer's journey.

For an insurance company, these are some example scenes:

A. Decide what kind of insurance policy is required or right for them.

B. Experience a near-miss accident.

C. Experience an accident and immediate aftermath.

D. Decide whether to make a claim and pay the deductible.

E. Make a claim and follow it through to conclusion.

Here are some different characters for the insurance company:

1. "Let This Be a Lesson"

2. "Downplay It"

3. "Poor Accident Record"

4. "Additional Protection Seeker"

The last two characters belong to purchasing-behavior segments, so they play a part in Scene A, but not in Scenes B or C. The first two are accident-behavior segments, so they don't show up in Scene A, and they're the stars of Scenes B and C. Try to broaden your cast of characters so they are appropriate to differing scenes.

Inspire Ideas

The patterns from the listening sessions are a rich matrix for collaborative idea generation. The important thing now is that you don't fall into the habit of claiming to know the solutions yourself.

Now is the time to stand upon your newly earned understanding of others. This includes your understanding of your peers' and stakeholders' purposes. Rather than latch on to an idea you think will support people better, latch on to your knowledge about those people and about the people you work with. Let other people lead the way, iterating through some ideas. To have any strength and hope of thriving, ideas need to be created collaboratively. Many heads are better than one, and an idea is always stronger when it gets bounced around a bit. See if the people you work with come up with the idea that was lurking at the back of your brain—make it a game—and watch if the ideas that get discussed don't surpass that lurker anyway. The importance of letting go of ownership of ideas and ideation is that you will be able to assess the value of ideas more clearly. This is part of the empathetic mindset.

Once you embrace the importance of not holding your ideas dear, then sure, go ahead and suggest ideas along with your peers. At this point, an idea is a seed that you're tossing out there with everyone else. It's one of many. Your responsibility lies in cultivating the spot where the seeds land, on cultivating a fertile understanding of the people you are trying to support. Your focus is on fostering that empathetic understanding throughout your organization. If the seeds of ideas land in such a rich environment, they can't help but sprout into much stronger seedlings than ideas that struggle in an environment where understanding is sparse or one-dimensional.

Additionally, the empathetic mindset can lessen political posturing. If two different groups have differing ideas, you can set the atmosphere by speaking neutrally, from your empathetic knowledge. Your experience of working through the listening sessions, summarizing, and observing patterns has effectively created a place in your mind full of other people's thinking. You can focus on representing that empathy. When you open your mouth, the people's voices come out, not your own.

Remind Yourself of Organizational Goals

As you dive into an idea-generation session, whether it's informal in the hallway or formal in a conference room, keep in mind your organizational goals for the year. You can remind yourself of the goals silently or out loud with your colleagues. You need this quick orientation for your creative thought process so you can choose patterns that are more related to the organization's priorities. You'll also be able to see where people's priorities split away, and whether that's significant to how you are currently deploying your resources in support of them.

Start by Describing a Pattern

To begin, simply state a few of the patterns and summaries. Describing a pattern aloud sets the stage and invites collaborators to join in. You can either keep the list of patterns and summaries handy or work from memory.

If you are doing this solo, conduct a little dialogue in your head. Stare off into space, imagining the scenes from the pattern. Some people say getting away from your usual surroundings will help you concentrate on this other person's thinking.[6]

First Person Pronoun "I"

The first guideline for this activity is that you should try to use the first person pronoun "I." Using empathy means putting yourself in someone else's shoes. When you say "he" or "she" for describing a person's thinking, you are using your own perspective to look at that person. You inadvertently erect a barrier and put yourself on the other side to watch the other person in the scenario like a movie. There's an extra filter in there. Using "I" tricks your mind into thinking more like the other person thinks.

---

6 See also Leah Buley's *The User Experience Team of One* for more advice for doing this solo. New York: Rosenfeld Media, 2013.

When you pepper the description of a pattern with quotes from people, the use of the personal pronoun "I" truly doesn't feel contrived. You can also get mileage out of the verbs you chose for the summaries.

No Need for Scenarios

If you have done ideation sessions before, you might have invented specific scenarios. You don't need to write scenarios anymore. Use the actual scenes you heard in the sessions and the actual thinking, reactions, and undercurrents from the scene.

Then let your collaborators extend the scene. It only takes a few seconds of thinking per direction. Try to help the group cycle through extensions that might end in various ways that your organization could support. And don't limit yourselves to a product or a service— explore things that might mean adjusting a process or writing new content, etc.

> **TIP** DESCRIBE IT TO SOMEONE
>
> If you work alone, you'll want to talk through your ideas with other people in your networks. These can be people outside of work, in professional groups, peers from previous jobs, etc. Describing an idea aloud to someone has a powerful, instantaneous clarifying effect. Describing an idea in writing to someone has a similar same effect.

Reasoning, Not Demographics

An even more important guideline for this activity is to avoid demographics entirely. Demographics are descriptors such as gender, age, income-level, health, religion, eye color, nationality, political-affiliation, and so on. To stay within an empathetic mindset, you need to concentrate on the reasoning patterns you found. Instead of talking about "people who are pre-diabetic," talk about the different reasoning you heard: "people who reach for sugary comfort foods out of habit," and "people who feel so busy they fall back on fast food," and "people who eat whatever their family and friends eat," if these happen to be your behavioral segments. This practice keeps you from making assumptions.

As another example, saying that a person belongs to a certain political group does not explain her reasoning and guiding principles. Indeed, a political label invites the assumption that this individual—and all individuals of the same demographic—align with your interpretation of some of the viewpoints of that party. Rarely do all individuals interpret a viewpoint in exactly the same way.

Assumptions are pernicious. You make them without knowing it. And they are usually wrong in at least one way. The empathetic mindset—concentrating on the deeper things you found about a person's thinking—will help you avoid assumptions, or at least recognize when you have misstepped.

In Western culture, using demographics as shorthand for people's thinking is widespread. You get hit with it in media, entertainment, professional presentations, and casual conversation. People make demographic statements without knowing it, or they make demographic statements as hyperbole. If you feel able, try pointing out these demographic assumptions when your collaborators mention them. When you hear someone say something like, "Prediabetics always think about sugar; they just can't get sweets out of their minds," it's your cue.

Even if a certain way of reasoning forms a strong trend within a demographic, do not use *the demographic label.* Correlation is not causation. A demographic, such as gender, is not causing a certain way of reasoning. It's the reasoning, not the demographic, that should influence how you decide to support people.[7]

Your boss might prod you to say something demographically significant about the patterns, which puts you in a delicate situation. Try to help everyone at your organization understand the empathic mindset by referring to specific people or to a reasoning-based behavioral segment instead of a demographic. Give people at your organization better words so they can wield the patterns you found without demographic assumptions (see Figure 6.5).

---

7 An example of the deleterious effects of demographic profiling appears in the *Wall Street Journal* Online Edition, The Middle Seat column, by Scott McCartney: "He Carries On; She Likes to Check," November 28, 2012; online.wsj.com. In research I did, the reasons for carrying bags on board were because of the value or vulnerability of the items, for speed leaving the airport at the destination, and because the airline had lost a person's checked bags in the past. These reasons transcended gender.

FIGURE 6.5

See if you can ask someone who just made a demographic statement to restate in terms of reasoning patterns you found.

Make Notes of the Ideas

As the ideas pile up and get prodded and molded into different shapes, take some notes so you can remember what was discussed later. Include mention of how ideas tie back to business advantages or organizational goals. Do not make anything more formal than notes. You've probably experienced the juggernaut that arises from formally written descriptions of ideas. The description becomes a document that either becomes too detailed to nimbly change as you rethink things, or the basic ideas get set in stone. Changes get brushed aside because it's just too hard to keep the formal document updated.

So make notes. Give ideas temporary working titles. Keep it shorter than you would normally. Then return to each idea a day or so later and discuss it again before starting on a sketch or prototype. A little time gives you tons of perspective and creative intuition.

Test How Well You Are Empathizing

Using actors as a kind of metric, you can assess how well you're doing with your own empathy. Actors empathize with the characters they represent. Any time you see a television show or a movie, you can recognize when an actor is good because the character is the only thing conveyed. When an actor isn't as skilled, you notice that the actor is bringing her own reactions to all the parts she plays. More than a few television shows[8] and movies have featured two characters experiencing a mind/body swap. It's a mark of the skill of the actors that they can convincingly portray the opposite character in the scene. When you state your "I" phrases, do you sound like the other person? Or, for instance, are you showing how you reason, or showing what your opinion of a person is by the tone of your voice?

If you are bold, you can act out scenes and even film yourself. Many people are a little embarrassed to do real, out-loud acting, though. There are some great workshops on the improvisation technique (improv) that can help you get into it if you want—improv is great for boosting creativity as a group. For those of you who don't want to act, it might feel a little immature, like a game of "pretend" that you outgrew long ago. Yet, despite all the awkward feelings, it can be a powerful way to get your mind into an empathic mode. Try it if your group is willing.

---

8 One of the earlier examples is *The Avengers*, "Who's Who???" where enemy agent Basil is swapped with John Steed, and then Mrs. Peel ends up being swapped with enemy agent Lola, 1967.

Another test of your level of empathizing is to write a screenplay, but of the inner train of thought for someone in a specific extended scene. This process of writing can help you think things through more clearly. Or write a comic strip with thought bubbles and stick figures.[9] Help the reader laugh or wince with the character. You can also use these materials to assist in your communication of the ideas beyond your team.

A third way to test your level of empathizing is to purposely reach out to the scenes that feel very alien from your own experiences. If you can voice someone's reasoning that you were previously unfamiliar with, or that you disagree with, then you are empathizing. "I don't trust the airline to set things right, so I confront the gate agent myself. I yell at her so she will realize the magnitude of her mistake and how much she has upset me." These might be sentiments that are very different from your own. If you are able to say them with conviction, and believe them just for the space of time that you are that character, then you are empathizing.

Check the Ideas

This is an initial trip around the Think-Make-Check cycle. Your empathy influenced your brainstorming during the Think stage. Now you'll want to help validate the ideas by reviewing them with others. To review, you'll need to communicate the ideas to others— "Make" the ideas take some sort of form. Your role, as representative of the people from the listening sessions, is to provide the stories that go along with the description or sketch of each idea. An idea without context is subject to misinterpretation.[10] Static documentation (e.g., wireframes, mock-ups, experience maps) needs a scenario or two, along with well-defined characters from the listening sessions or personas. Dynamic communications (e.g., prototypes and interactive mock-ups) need the story and personas, too. For someone to behold its significance, you need to point out a few paths through the interaction. Use the voices you have collected to tell these stories. Once you have made something of your idea that others can understand, then you can "Check" it with them.

---

9 Kevin Cheng's book *See What I Mean* (Rosenfeld Media) is a good guide, as is Scott McCloud's book *Understanding Comics* (William Morrow).

10 "A wireframe without a context is meaningless. It doesn't represent the design, nor does a clickable prototype ... we need to do both—design and tell the story." Marcin Treder, "UX for Startups: Lesson 4. Design Is About Telling the Story, Isn't It?" *UX Pin Newsletter*, September 2013.

As a final test of an idea before investing any resources in it, create a parallel version of the story where your idea does not exist, but the characters still achieve their intent. This parallel version is a great way to clarify your story and single out which thinking and reactions you are trying to support in particular.

What About Ideas Already Underway?

What if some patterns cause you to realize something needs to change in the way you already support people? It's completely reasonable to reshape ideas already in discussion, development, or use—it just might take your skill and dedication to persuade people that it will make a positive difference (see Chapter 7). If you've done the work it takes to forge a collaborative environment, then this task will be easier.

On the other hand, you might encounter someone in leadership who has a special interest in going a particular direction she has envisioned. But, based on your deep understanding of the people's reasoning, you see a flaw in her plan. Try a little experiment by stepping through an extended scene of this leader's vision, expressing the character's thoughts aloud. You can test if the idea either won't help any of the characters effectively or will frustrate them. Or you might surprise yourself and discover that your initial misgivings don't really play out, and the leader's idea is sound.

In the former case, you can then ask to have a discussion with the decision-maker or her direct reports. You can demonstrate how your leader's plan might go awry, not by expressing your opinion, but by running through the extended scene with the voices of people from your listening sessions. This kind of discussion, without opinions, usually results in progress.

Of course, some leaders believe so fervently in their idea that they perceive a request to have a meeting as an attack on the energy which they need to breathe life into their idea. They're already staying up late, and working when everyone else is taking a break. Listen to them, step into their shoes, feel their energy and thinking. Show them you are interested. Eventually, you will be able to collaborate.

Solve for More

The assumption is that when you find a pattern across people, the pattern is something that everyone might like support with. The opposite could be true: one set of individuals may have a pattern that requires completely different support than another group's pattern. For example, one pattern might depict people wanting time and space to solve a problem, whereas another pattern might show the need for frequent conversation and updates while solving a problem. Clearly, you will want to support each pattern differently.

When an organization takes the time, it can really sharpen its tactics for supporting people this way. By defining the most prevalent or profitable patterns, it can spotlight whom it wants to support. It can follow a tighter path to development, rollout, and maintenance of an idea. It can put in exactly the right amount of effort toward exactly the right audience for this particular timeframe.

Most of the ways you solve things stem from your own perspective. This is axiomatic, because you're the one doing the solving. So you make an effort to bring other people's perspectives to bear. The problem is, there's an awful lot of pressure out there to hurry up and make something. It's not like you can push back on everyone at the organization. So push back on yourself first. As you are making decisions about the things you make, try this trick. Just like reporters are supposed to cite three sources for a fact, and like homeowners are supposed to get three estimates for repair work, run your brain through three different perspectives (see Figure 6.6). You can do this in a matter of a few minutes. The three perspectives can be from similar behavioral groups or from dissimilar ones. Running through three other perspectives helps you make adjustments to your ideas so that they are even stronger. You don't want people at your organization to fall into the trap of laying out something for themselves, because they, themselves, are not the target behavioral segment.

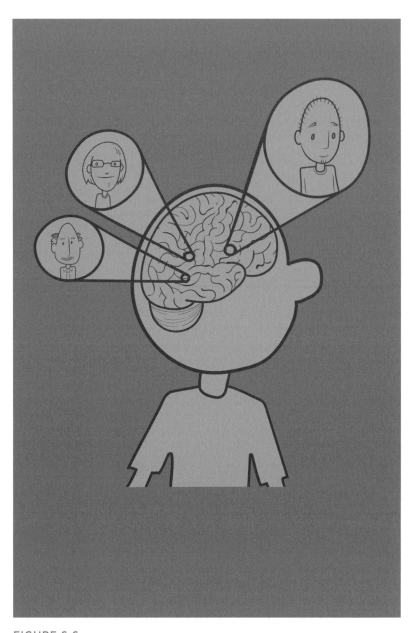

FIGURE 6.6

Take a few minutes to run through at least three other people's perspectives as you polish your idea.

Explore Varied Combinations

Humans are diverse. No one approach of yours will work for everyone—that's a given. What you make might need to be split into a couple of different solutions, suited to different behavior patterns. Or different paths through one solution might be appropriate. Written content, a service, a product, policy, or a process can each be split into different instances. Without studying the possible angles, your organization runs the risk of making something that either unconsciously fits one reasoning pattern or fits none of the reasoning patterns well.

You can't make 100 permutations of a similar service. But you can make two versions. Or three. This does not mean doubling or tripling your effort, because your offering works the same way under the hood. It's the way a person accesses your offering that changes from version to version. The wording and tone might change. Emphasis might change. While this does take a lot of work, it certainly doesn't take *twice* as much work.

Look for Enduring Directions

There is an argument for making your offerings sustainable—things that are extensible, that you don't toss aside, but instead keep for a long time. Take a look at the buzzwords that are still in use, such as "new," "brand new," and "new and improved." Organizations reissue the same basic offering with small tweaks to guarantee continued purchases, profits, and patents. You might even suspect companies of purposely bloating your phone, slowing it down, in an attempt to make you upgrade. With the empathy you developed for customers, you might be able to help your organization sustain profits not through purchase and repurchase, but through attracting people away from the competition with well-thought-out details or with ideas that support subsets of your audience more closely. Or by reusing existing components in more powerful, creative, or personal ways. (Do this internally, too, because you don't want your organization to be an instance of the cobbler's children having no shoes.)

When you are working out solutions, you may end up having a discussion about an important question, "How much do we care about this subgroup?" For example, the group in question may have never encountered your organization before and will never encounter it again, so there's no long-term relationship. Should you purposely ignore these one-encounter kinds of people? What percentage of your overall metrics are they? It may be hard to let go of an audience which is a favorite, but which isn't a good direction for your organization at the moment. Nonetheless, this discussion is helpful. Be honest and open with yourselves. How many organizations have crumpled because of just this simple reluctance to be clear about whom they are supporting?

You don't have to stop development or give up on a great idea just because the answers to these questions mean the people you are supporting are a minority. If that is whom you really want to support, and it makes sense from a commitment point of view for your organization, then great! You've just taken the first step toward more streamlined tactics. The admission that you're not focused on the other audiences gives you permission to focus better on the first group.

A big assumption is in operation: convincing someone to decide to buy is the key goal. For services that are free, advertising other things for sale or getting a cut of the transaction is what provides the revenue stream.[11] This big assumption has filtered into Western culture: aggregate groups are largely referred to as *consumers*, mythically using every moment of their days to make purchases. Perhaps you can find ways to branch out beyond consumerism.

Solve More Than Surface-Level Problems

If your organization evaluates how well your offerings support people, especially on a recurring basis, you probably have a lot of data that has guided the changes you have made. These data generally trend up, pointing in an encouraging direction. The people you

---

11 When Viv, "the global brain," was announced, the scenario used to explain it was finding a bottle of wine to buy that would go well with lasagna, since you're on your way to your brother's house for dinner.

support seem pretty happy with the offering. But these measurements miss the fact that it is second nature for humans to make adjustments—in other words, to make do with situations and tools that are less than perfect. Humans adapt. So the metrics only show humans making your offering work, or making work-arounds to allow the offering space in their lives.

The error probably lies in defining scenarios that are too pat. Human reasoning is complex and easily interconnects across different systems, constructs, and people. People are governed by biology. People also take different paths to arrive at your offering. Don't assume everyone arrived for the same reason or using the same decisions. Try for actual scenarios from the people you heard from. Represent interwoven ecosystems. Extend these scenarios with edge cases that might be common. Then try to solve each one of them holistically, rather than in discrete steps.

Example: Sending Your Nephew a Belated Birthday Card

In the "Jelly Bean" version of Android, there is a widget called "Weather" that you can put on your home screen. The widget also shows the time and date, and it shows a little birthday cake if someone in your contact list has a birthday that day. Presumably, the engineers expected you would be able to remember whose birthday it was, as the cake icon does not include the name of the person celebrating.

If you have lots of people in your contact list, and you don't remember whose birthday the icon represents, you must open up a separate calendar application to find out. It turns out that it's your nephew's birthday, so you decide to send a belated paper card to him, so you can include a little gift. You get out a card, write a little note, and realize you need to look up his address. The birthday notation in the calendar does not have a link back to the contact. You have to use a third application, your contact list, to look up the home address to write on the envelope. None of these apps link the birthday directly to any of the other data.

This scenario is a clear example of how the people creating the apps did not think things through from a perspective different than their own, where they know whose birthday it is.

Keep in Mind Whom You Are Addressing

Inevitably, you'll find yourself in a scenario where someone makes a blanket statement like, "Everyone searches by keyword. So let's treat email that way." This is your opportunity to ask, "Who is *everyone*, exactly? Who benefits?" Help the people around you to make a decision with their eyes wide open. You can delineate exactly which part of the audience you want to address, when, and why.

> **TIP** BEWARE OF THESE PHRASES
>
> Let these words be red flags of warning when you hear them in your own conference room.
>
> - *Everyone* does it.
> - It's *easier* to do it this way.
> - It's *better* to do it this way.

Especially in writing, but also in policies, services, and products, what you create can so easily rub a person the wrong way. The way you word things or the categories and definitions you create about the people you support—these have the potential to be off-putting. Moreover, the lack of attention to a certain subtype of person can make those people have emotional reactions. Maybe they're not turning away from your organization, but don't count that as a success. It might simply be that "there's no other option."

For example, an eBay member might be active in bursts. During one of her inactive periods, she happens to move from one city to another. Her landline and email have both changed, and she did not register a mobile number with her account. The password reset function at eBay depends upon one of these things staying constant (see Figure 6.7). The organization either didn't think about this particular situation or decided it wasn't important enough to address directly. The next steps make the member feel ignored, anxious, and overwhelmed—none of which are emotions eBay wants to foster in its members.

The addition of text acknowledging this situation goes a long way toward supporting the member and not causing these emotions. "None of these contact methods up-to-date anymore? Please call this number." Don't send this member to a generic page with "contact customer support," where the text implies that her safety and security are at risk. Moreover, don't accuse the member of "having trouble," or indicate that she might "need more help." These phrases imply the member is not smart enough to do what she wants to do. Phrases like "Password reset not working?" and "How can we support you?" imply the fault is with the service, not the member, which is what you want. Take the blame for the problem so that you don't cause negative emotions and reactions.

Get an email
We'll send a link to
g****v@sbcglobal.net

Get a text
We'll text you at (530)-xxx-xx52*
with a PIN

Get a call
We'll call you at (530)-xxx-xx52*
with a PIN

Having trouble resetting your password? register for a new account or contact customer support
* By selecting this method, you agree to receive text or pre-recorded message to this number. Cell charges may apply.

FIGURE 6.7
If you've moved and have a new email address and phone number, this password-reset page from eBay only fills you with dread about long hold-times on the customer support line, or worse, losing your history and standing if you have to set up a new account.

Solve for the End Customer

Plenty of organizations make things for a company who then uses that solution to serve *their* customers. These organizations have begun experimenting with a focus on the end customers, in addition to the people who directly acquire their offering. This means finding out more about the patterns of behavior in these end customers—a step that is sometimes met with fear by the direct customer that the organization is bypassing them. Sometimes, the situation requires working together with the direct customer to understand the end customer better. You should help everyone involved to identify and separate the different behavioral audiences you are addressing.

Practice These Skills

Making use of the knowledge you've collected requires actually dwelling on that knowledge for a bit. Making this a separate step from your brainstorming session can be helpful. It may seem like it would bloat the whole process you follow, but it only takes 15 minutes.

Practice: Design-less Design Session

A good practice to fall into is to begin any design work with a "pre-session" where you simply discuss the people and scenes that relate to the idea you are exploring. It can be a short session. During this discussion of the people you've heard from, refrain completely from sketching solutions or details of a design component. You may sketch scenarios and flow or journeys that a person may take to achieve her purpose. Remain solution agnostic during this "pre-session."

Summary

To create something, you benefit from understanding the patterns of how various people reason. There will be differences and similarities that you can form into behavioral groups. Maybe you are not directly responsible for coming up with new ideas for your organization or maybe you are. But no matter what, you're not in it alone. Creating new ideas and shaping them requires other minds to help influence your thinking. As the person who is the skilled listener—the person who represents the patterns you discovered across the people you hope to support—you are perfectly positioned to facilitate this collaboration.

Understand where the team members are coming from and help each person feel confident coming up with concepts. Support each person with stories from your empathy work. Maintain team cooperation by showing people how to let go of ownership of their idea and embrace the next person's modification.

LOOK FOR PATTERNS

- **Quick Method:** Seek patterns by memory.
- **Rich Method:** Look for patterns across summaries.
    - Consider one summary at a time.
    - Wrap your mind around the difficult ones.
    - Assess your confidence.

CREATE BEHAVIORAL SEGMENTS FROM THE PATTERNS

- Group people with similar patterns of reasoning.
- Behavioral segments first, and then maybe personas.
- It's a rotating cast.

INSPIRE IDEAS

- Remind yourself of organizational goals.
- Start by describing a pattern.
- First-person pronoun "I."
- No need for scenarios.
- Reasoning, not demographics.
- Make notes of the ideas.
- Test how well you are empathizing.

SOLVE FOR MORE

- Explore varied combinations.
- Look for enduring directions.
- Keep in mind whom you are addressing.
- Solve for the end customer.

When your boss gives you a request,
find out the deeper purpose
of what he means.

Apply Empathy with People at Work

Every so often, you'll start work in the morning full of ambition for the day, only to find that a coworker is having a fit about the way something was done. Or maybe someone in leadership has requested that you drop everything to pursue something else. So much for the immense progress you intended to make before evening. Instead, your time goes toward understanding the changes, the political currents, and the gossip about who feels what about the whole thing. It's inevitable—so much of your day goes toward interacting with other people.[1] And that's never going to change, because organizations are made up of people. It's better to embrace the humanity of the people you work with than to expect the efficiency and productivity you might have if people weren't people.

The halts in progress at work happen because, among other reasons, people at all levels of the hierarchy have not invested time in understanding one another. For example, if a coworker is having a fit, the reason is often rooted in others not understanding or appreciating his ideas, or because another person encroached on his area of decision-making. Nevertheless, monthly productivity reports focus on the things you get done, not on how well you relate to others. Yearly performance reviews include perhaps a small piece that evaluates your ability to collaborate. But earning the trust of people at work, understanding what drives people, deciding what to say and what to request—all these require empathy. Learning how your coworkers reason and then acting on this knowledge is paramount to your productivity. It won't bring it up to superhuman levels, but it will reduce the frequency and duration of the halts.

You can't apply empathy unless you've taken time to develop it. When you have developed empathy with the people around you at work, your improved understanding will change the way you see things and the way you speak to people. It raises your awareness and subconsciously shifts your own thinking.

---

1 Business journals and consultants (e.g., *American Journal of Business*, "Total Quality Management," Peter Drucker, Edward Shaw) rail against "wasted time" in measuring white-collar productivity. Systems are devised to identify these gaps and close them, much like what was done in labor and manufacturing.

Collaborate with People

You rarely get to choose whom you will collaborate with at work. Whether you've worked together before or not, the empathetic mindset allows you to adopt a deliberate and intentional manner in approaching your collaborators. In order to rely on your fellow employees as you work, you need to build up trust. You want to be aware of any emotional reactions so that you can see and address the root causes of difficulties, rather than lob accusations and complaints back and forth, or worse—avoid communication.

When lack of empathy is widespread, working within a broken culture feels awful. You try to do the right thing, but instead you witness everything spiral out of control. You might not even have any control in the first place. Maybe no one has power, or the people in power don't seem to want to spend any time listening to anyone. When this is the case, a lot of people simply give up on projects, jobs, and even careers because of failed collaboration. It doesn't have to be you.

Perennial Listening

If you spend a portion of your time listening to your peers, absorbing their motivations and intentions, you can develop the empathy you need. Since you'll be seeing the same people again and again in your work, listening will be an ongoing project. It will also be informal—seize an opportunity to listen when it presents itself (see Figure 7.1), but don't always put yourself in "listening mode" when you are with each person. And, as a reminder, "each person" means that these opportunities need to be isolated from other coworkers. If the opportunity arises face-to-face, but you are with others, wait for another time when you and the other person can talk privately. Be on the lookout for opportunities by phone as well. Email can work, too, as long as you are extra careful about what you write, lest it be misconstrued.

Understanding the perspectives of the people you interact with will help you adjust what you say and how you collaborate. The goal is not to persuade others to adopt your intentions. The goal is to let empathy affect your own approach. Additionally, be conscious of what you say to people. Remember the first rule of critique: If you want to say something negative, make yourself say something positive first. The neutral mindset will help you acknowledge each person's intentions and work to improve the relationship—not necessarily toward the direction of liking each other, but toward the direction of being able to capitalize upon each other's input to the work.

FIGURE 7.1
Seize every opportunity with individual coworkers to listen to what's on their minds.

TIP TAKE TURNS

Maybe two of you are simultaneously interested in developing empathy. It doesn't work well when both of you try listening at the same time. If you're trying to understand the other person when the other person is trying to understand you, conversation is likely to stay shallow, falter, or even fall into argument. Decide who is listening for the interval; then give yourselves a break before you switch roles. The break will give you both time to digest what was said.

This same approach works with your project stakeholders and clients. Find out their concerns. Dig into the reasons behind their requests or reactions. Balance showing them that you know what you're doing with intervals of listening. The more you demonstrate how deeply you want to understand them, the more they'll trust and respect you. They are as much your collaborators as your peers.

Act Like a Pollinator

Bees and butterflies pollinate flowers so plants can produce fruit—however, the bees and butterflies don't think of themselves as pollinators. They're more interested in visiting every flower they can. They just happen to pick up a little pollen at one plant and deposit it at another. A part of collaborating with people is similar—spreading what you and others have discovered around, so everyone can rise together. The knowledge you have to offer is the empathy you develop with people that the organization supports. This empathy will be more useful if you spread it around.

Visiting people, in-person or remotely, is what's key. There are some organizations that follow a tradition of report-writing as a method of spreading knowledge, but it's unlikely your coworkers will read a report. Some organizations recast the content of reports in other hopefully more compelling formats, such as video, but the same problem still applies. Unless your coworkers guess in advance the value of the content, they won't make the time to look at it. You can't send a report around to everyone's desk and expect it to make them excited about something.[2] That is a manifestly human activity.

There are all sorts of ways to spread knowledge around. You can orchestrate a social event every now and then, to expose employees at your organization to the people whom they are serving. You can make a short presentation at a company meeting. You and your team can individually have coffee, lunch, or a short call with different key people across divisions. Each of these examples is intended to help others develop empathy through the use of already-gathered stories.[3]

---

2 Nate Bolt, former Design Research Manager at Facebook, says, "We try to never deliver any reports ever … reports can't attend meetings, and they can't argue in favor of their findings." *Fast Company Labs*, "Secrets from Facebook's Mobile UX Testing Team," by Jay Cassano, April 8, 2013.

3 Many organizations host presentations to help other divisions take advantage of what they've learned about people. CaptitalOne, General Electric, Rackspace, and Yahoo! have all started programs for this kind of knowledge sharing.

Whatever approach to spreading knowledge you decide to use, keep in mind that a lot of people at your organization will be focused on how well the product or service works, not on how well people can achieve their purpose. Share knowledge clearly so that peers know the focus is on people, not product. It wouldn't be surprising to hear someone echo what you hear at a project debriefing, "We've done all this research, and I didn't learn anything new about our *product*. But, after 25 years in the business, now I can look at my *customers* and see them from a different viewpoint."[4]

If you're an introvert, getting in front of people may sound challenging. So don't. Get beside them at a desk or go to lunch with them. You know where you personally feel comfortable, so come up with a way to have chats with folks. If you are passionate about what you've learned from people, let that passion burn past your natural reticence. Be the evangelist for the concepts you heard in the listening sessions. You don't have to stand up in front of a room full of people.

Think of yourself as a resource for everyone at the organization. You're the walking, talking embodiment of all the people (internal or external) the team is trying to support. When you open your mouth, their voices come out. You've heard plenty of stories where something surprising catalyzes an integral change. (The nurse who looks at a situation from the patient's view and suggests something the doctor wouldn't have thought to try.) Spread the stories to as many cracks and crevices in your organization as you can find. It's a good side project, and it will bring you into contact with more and more people who will remember you for reaching out.

Lead a Team

If you are a manager of a team, you are responsible for nurturing creativity. Creativity and new approaches can have more impact on the success of your organization than productivity alone. Digital products, in-person services, policy-making, process design, and writing all hinge upon originality, functionality, sustainability, and the human touch, not simply time-to-complete. Productivity by itself

---

4 Patrick DiMichele, Manifest Digital, client usability debrief.

is the core concern of managers who produce things using human *labor*, but managers who rely on human *minds* have this additional responsibility of nurturing. Creativity relies on amassing knowledge, sharing inputs, letting inspiration strike, and working through ideas together. To help your team work well together, you are responsible for teaching relationship- and trust-building through your own practice and individual coaching.

More Perennial Listening

Developing empathy in a leadership position means developing an understanding of how each person on your team reasons and what drives his decisions. It means knowing what will upset his concentration and what will energize his mind. Applying empathy as a leader means choosing your words so they do the least harm and making requests with the other person's perspective and purpose in mind. It also means pointing the person in a direction that will increase his skills or awareness.

To this end, pursue a regular schedule of formal listening sessions with each person on your team. Informal, unscheduled sessions are also okay, but having this practice in place lets your team know that developing empathy to engender collaboration skills is an important part of your agenda with them. As usual, during the sessions you want to remain neutral with ideas, letting the team member lead the discussion. You can give broad guidelines to get things started, but remind yourself to stick to understanding this person's reasoning, not explaining your own intentions. Try not to let your own urges overcome this neutrality.

Measuring Your Effectiveness Over Time

Summaries of the concepts in the sessions aren't required because you aren't comparing between team members. However, summaries can serve as a metric after each successive round of listening, to see how each team member has changed so that you can measure the effectiveness of your cultivation. Based on the progress shown in the notes, you can intentionally shift how you support each person until it fits better.

At a small biotech research company, one of the directors of the company, Jiyun, promoted a member of the staff, Rick, to become the group leader for a project. This was Rick's first experience as a group leader. Within two weeks, Jiyun was hearing from members of Rick's group that she needed to intervene. Rick was apparently treating other members of the team like lackeys, getting annoyed because people weren't doing what he wanted, refusing to do work that didn't suit him, hiding, not communicating, and handing off tasks instead of working with the team. In other words, he wasn't *leading*. The team was upset.

Jiyun's first impulse was to take over leadership of the group herself, because it would be easier. She could say to Rick, "Here's how you lead. Watch me." However, she realized this solution wouldn't truly help Rick become a leader, and worse, it might cause him embarrassment. Plus, she hadn't heard his side of the story. So she asked to meet with him about his leadership of the group, making sure he had ample time to put his thoughts and complaints in order before they were face-to-face.

During the meeting, she began by thanking him for some of his prior good work. Then she asked how the project was going. She stayed neutral and listened closely. It turns out, Rick was feeling really overloaded. He said people didn't listen to him and went off and did the wrong thing, making him spend twice as long with them explaining what he needed. He said his team wasn't being efficient, and that they would bring him problems that added to his workload. He was ending up doing everything himself.

Jiyun realized that the magnitude of his agitation was a lot higher than she expected. Perhaps she'd assigned too much work, with deadlines too close,

Culture

Team culture is a tricky thing. On the one hand, if everyone likes working together, creativity and productivity both go up. On the other hand, having too homogeneous a culture leads to group think: forgetting to be aware of other perspectives than what the group has in common. It also leads to rejection of people who do not share preferences and opinions, and to outright discrimination.[5]

---

5 "'Cultural Fit' Is a Shitty Excuse for Marginalizing Women in Tech," Valleywag, August 23, 2013.

for a new group leader. In her response, she began by acknowledging that he was under too much pressure. She apologized for not starting him out with an interval of a smaller workload, so he could find his balance. Even though the projects and deadlines were important to the company, she emphasized to him that his role as a leader and facilitator were more valuable in the long term. She also told Rick that she did not want to step in and have any involvement in the project. It was his responsibility. And she'd like to meet with him every other day to talk about how the leadership role was going.

At the next meeting, Rick came up with some great process ideas and asked questions about the needs and roles of the other team members. He asked how he should respond when people asked him questions that he couldn't answer. Jiyun was really pleased to see that he was starting to think about his role as a leader instead of acting like he had to do all the work himself. They discussed answers to his questions, and the meeting ended on a really positive note.

The next day, as Jiyun was walking through the building, she noticed Rick and his team discussing a project in the break room. She could see by their faces and body language that things were going better. Later that day, she asked a few of the team members how things were going. "Night and day," they said. "I don't know what you said to him, but it's made 100% difference." Jiyun was pleased that she'd kept neutral in the situation and had learned where Rick was coming from. She was pleased she'd given Rick the freedom to think of his own ideas about how to lead the people in that group, rather than just telling him what to do. Instead, he tapped in to his own good skills and behavior—exactly the things that caused Jiyun to promote him to group leader in the first place.

To avoid falling into this trap, go deeper than preferences and opinions. Look at guiding principles, and you'll find there is a lot more in common at the root level than at the level of preferences and opinions. Encourage people to search for deeper connections

Alternatively, team members may have different guiding principles. A guiding principle like "If you have to ask for help, don't put too much pressure on the person you're asking" could be the root of rocky relations between two coworkers. The coworker being asked feels pressure. His guiding principle subconsciously causes him to push back on his coworker. He wonders, "Is it really a crisis? You say almost everything is a crisis." Exposing this difference in principles can help the other coworker ask for help in a different manner.

By figuring out what makes your team members tick, you can build a team culture where they get the cognitive and emotional support they need to be creative. Culture can't be forced.[6]

Understand Your Higher-Ups

Executives at your organization may be clear about the direction of your combined efforts, but have they communicated the depth and philosophy of it clearly? In most cases, they have communicated clearly—to their direct reports. But once the message moves down the hierarchy, the clarity and depth of focus become lost. Like the game you played as a child, passing a whispered message around a circle of friends, the accuracy of the message depends upon communication skills and each person's awareness of his assumptions. In some cases, the executives don't communicate the reasoning behind their decisions, but savvy direct reports ferret it out on behalf of everyone else at the organization. In other instances, no one at the organization can really articulate why decisions were made.

Search for the Reasoning

No matter where you are in the hierarchy, it is important to know the underlying purpose of a directive so that your creativity, innovation, and collaboration will benefit. If you don't personally understand the reasoning behind any organizational decision, you owe it to your professional standing to find out. If *you are* the person who is making the guiding decisions, writing down the reasoning and guiding principles behind it will help you clearly communicate these deeper intentions.

If you're not the decision-maker, then you'll need to reach out to the hierarchy above you to find out. The decision-makers in your organization may be inaccessible.[7] There actually might be rules about who can impinge on an executive's time, in order to protect that leader from unnecessary details that his direct reports should be handling. So find the right person who may know the deeper reasoning and ask.

You can start with a query like, "So I can better support the <insert direction here>, can you tell me more about the thinking behind it?" If that probe doesn't yield rich answers, you can add questions about

---

6 On employee engagement," Meld Studios Blog: Our Thoughts, July 17, 2014. www.meldstudios.com.

7 See *It's Our Research* (Ch. 1), Tomer Sharon. New York: Morgan Kauffman, 2012.

the decision-maker's concerns and risks he is facing. If no one you ask has these answers, then you'll want to campaign for someone higher up to collect it—someone closer to the executives. The knowledge is important for everyone to be able to support the organization in the best way possible.

Decision-makers at the top are concerned with the longevity of the organization, as they should be. Deeply understanding the people your organization supports is secondary for them; in reverse, understanding the people you support is primary for you, and the success of the organization is secondary. There are details that are necessary to pursue for each objective. Getting to the purpose underneath the details of what your organization is doing might be an ongoing process, depending on how much your organization changes each year. It may benefit you to conduct ongoing listening sessions with your decision-makers.

What you find out, in the end, is that you are understanding where your leaders are coming from, and it changes the way you approach your work (see Figure 7.2).

FIGURE 7.2
People will work from different perspectives of a stated goal, unless the underlying purpose beneath a decision is communicated clearly.

Pushing Back Is Not Rebellion—It's Collaboration

You probably want your organization to succeed so that the people it supports gain from it and you can continue to work there. When you receive a task from decision-makers, it makes sense to understand the request as deeply as you can so that your work produces the best possible outcome. Too often, requests get accepted at face value, along with all the assumptions that stand in for actual discussion. Ideation and work cycle around the request without much broad insight. Like the story of the Chinese emperor's court, it would empower more people if you build the canal system not the tower to heaven. It is more powerful to exhibit understanding than competence. The empathetic mindset is not focused on oneself or one's own abilities.

Prod each request you receive to understand where it came from. Maybe your decision-maker has asked you to write a newsletter about specific topics. Why the newsletter? What is his purpose? Questioning someone to get more information about what is driving the request is not a form of disrespect, it is collaboration. You can discuss the intent behind the newsletter and explore what supports the people it is intended for. Do this with deference and respect for the decision-maker, who has reasons for his request, and together you may come to a different conclusion. You will envision richer approaches to the topic he wants to communicate.

Embrace your role as a member of the team responsible for the success of the people your organization supports, as well as for the continued success of your organization.

Know Yourself

The hardest part of working with people is remembering that your own reactions and attempts to communicate can have unintended consequences. It's futile to try to stop yourself from having reactions entirely, but you can certainly aim to understand the circumstances and triggers that cause your reactions. Being able to simply name them will help you dampen their effects and put your purpose back at the center of your focus. It can then help you clarify the way you communicate with others.

NOTE 故曰：知彼知己，百戰不殆；不知彼而知己，
一勝一負；不知彼，不知己，每戰必殆。

So it is said that if you know your enemies and know yourself,
you can win a hundred battles without a single loss.

If you only know yourself, but not your opponent, you may win
or may lose.

If you know neither yourself nor your enemy, you will always
endanger yourself.[8]

—Sun Tzu, military general, strategist, philosopher

As Sun Tzu said, half the equation for avoiding danger is knowing
yourself. How can you untangle or decode your own motivations?
One approach is to try looking for the same three kinds of things in
your own reasoning that you look for in listening sessions: thinking,
reactions, and guiding principles. See if something you're communicating is a preference or an opinion; recognize if it's conjecture.
Try to spot when you are speaking in generalities or focusing on
explanation. Using these metrics, you can become a little more aware
of what you express to others. You can add to these a description of
your deeper reasoning, making the meaning of your communication
more forthright.

Another skill to develop is being aware when another person is having an emotional reaction during an interaction with you. This talent
is a little harder because first of all, it occurs during discussion with
someone you work with, so you might be anxious or embarrassed
about trying. Second, recognition always occurs at least a few beats
after the other person expresses his emotion. When you do recognize
it, you have the chance to slow down and ask the other person about
his emotion. If he needs it, give him permission to withdraw from
the situation until later. Recognizing another person's emotion helps
you manage your interaction with that person.[9] You will be better
prepared to keep yourself on track.

---

8 Wikipedia entry for *The Art of War* written by Sun Tzu over 2200 years ago.

9 The psychological practice of "cognitive therapy" teaches patients to recognize
   that thoughts lead to emotions, and emotions lead to thoughts.

Finally, at an interpersonal level, examine your intentions. Are you participating as a team member, or as someone who is trying to be at the head of his class? An apt analogy is playing an instrument in an orchestra. Much of what you play is in support of another instrument, and different instruments switch roles and play the lead. Nonetheless, all the musicians focus on the power and emotion of what you are creating for the audience. If you're more sports-inclined, the team metaphor works as well. You pass the ball to the person best situated to help the team score. Understanding your teammates and encouraging them when it's their turn to do their thing—this is empathy playing out in your interactions. This kind of empathy can help not only between team members, but also across divisions within your organization.

Practice These Skills

Becoming more intentional in how you interact with people at work is not something that's going to happen overnight, no matter how much you wish it would. Try out some of the ideas in these practices.

Practice 1: Know Yourself

Listening to *yourself* is an additional way of practicing your empathetic mindset so that later you can draw forth similar clarity from people you listen to. Moreover, when you acknowledge the role that emotions play in your own reasoning, you can identify emotions more easily in others.

Here's a chance to practice self-awareness. Think of a recent event you were involved in where things didn't go as you expected. Things could have gone worse, or better, or simply in a different direction. It doesn't have to be an important event. Anything will work: you heard some surprising family news, you were involved in a difference of opinion, you accidentally broke something, or you had a problem at a restaurant, for example.

On a blank page, make three sections and put these three headings at the top of each section: Thinking, Reactions, and Guiding Principles. Then try to remember as many details about the event that you can and write down your internal "thinking process" as the episode unfolded. You don't have to keep everything you write in chronological order.

If you feel like it, add columns for any of these other types: opinion, preference, explanation, generality, passive behavior, and conjecture. See what parts of your thinking and speaking fall into those columns. It's not "bad" to have entries in those columns—it just means you need to work on giving greater depth and clarity to the entries in the next event you experience. You want to focus on putting more concepts in the Thinking, Reactions, or Guiding Principles columns.

Example: Miles' Story of "When Things Did Not Go as Expected"

At the time, Miles was a member of a research team, even though his background was in visual design. The research team was made up of people from two companies that merged, and Miles was excited to be part of a team exploring a deeper understanding of the people the company served. Miles had scheduled a listening session, and this was only his second time using the conference call system. The first time he used the conference system, it had been a confusing and frustrating experience. Luckily, other team members were on that first call and started the recording for him, so he could concentrate on the person instead of the technology. However, this particular day, no one else from the team could join him to help, even though they had agreed to. He was concerned that he would end up failing to make the conference system work, thereby inconveniencing the customer.

Afterward, listing his thoughts and reactions helped Miles put his emotions in perspective. It also showed him that he behaved according to his principles during the event, which reestablished his sense of worth. Here are the things that went through Miles's mind as the morning unfolded (see Figure 7.3).

Thinking

- Decide that, as call moderator, I am in the driver's seat and it's my decision whether to proceed with the call to the customer
- Choose to call the customer to reschedule because I am not certain I can get the recording to work, and a call with no recording is worthless
- Describe the situation as a temporary recording technology problem so the customer doesn't think of us as unprofessional
- Let my other team members know I have rescheduled with the customer

Reactions

- Feel annoyed that team members are not available to take part in the scheduled research call, as they had promised
- Feel confident about conducting a research call, but not the conference system behind it
- Feel embarrassed that I haven't taken the time to resolve my insecurities about the conference system
- Feel relieved that the customer is gracious about the request for a reschedule and we are able to agree on a new date and time

Guiding Principles

- Work with a situation as it is, not as it was supposed to be
- Treat our customer's time as a very valuable commodity
- Represent our company in a professional way when talking to customers, so I don't waste her time
- Show up when I say I will (knowing this is not always possible because things do happen)
- Take the hit when something goes wrong, if it's the best way to smooth things over or prevent ill will
- Stand up for myself

FIGURE 7.3

Here are the lists that Miles wrote after the morning at work when things did not go as planned. These lists helped him feel better about how he handled things.

Practice 2: Begin to Understand Your Decision-Makers

If you want a deeper understanding of the purpose behind what you are asked to do, you need to hear the reasoning from the person who makes the decisions. You need to be able to ask for clarification. You can gather this understanding either directly from this person (from his direct reports) or further down the chain (if he has been successful at explaining his reasoning to them). Don't let your assumptions about those people higher up in the hierarchy stop you from getting clarification about purposes. You need this understanding so that you can support this person with your best work.

1. List people who give you work requests. They don't necessarily have to be your immediate manager, especially if that manager is simply relaying orders. If you don't know *who they are*, start asking around.

2. Find out from your peers whether each of these people has been willing to explain the detailed purpose of a request to anyone else. You want to know if any one of them has a closed-door policy, so you know what to expect and what others have experienced.

3. Find out where these people spend their time. If any one of them is in a location far from your own, you're facing a bigger challenge to establish a collaborative relationship. You will probably need to rely on remote conversations.

4. Find out who tends to meet with these people. Your goal is to find out who might have already done your work for you—asking the person details about his purpose for each request. If someone has already done this, you can collaborate directly with this person, going back to the requestor if you both come up against alternatives that need clarification.

5. If no one else plays this role with the requestor, then you can advertise that you need more in-depth information to better support the request. You will end up either working with a person in between you and the requestor in the hierarchy, or you'll have a chance to meet a few times with the requestor himself to gather deeper information. There is also a chance you'll be somehow forbidden from getting clarification. If this last scenario comes true, then keep asking good, solid questions about the purpose of the request, to demonstrate the kind of knowledge you need in order to better execute the request.

6. If it seems likely you will get time with someone much higher up, find out how he prefers to approach his meetings. Prepare for the meeting, doing your best to read everything you can find about this leader and his perspective and history.[10] This meeting is about understanding intentions with someone who has limited time; you want to see what you can learn about the other person's thinking via what has been written first.

Summary

The empathic mindset can be applied to the people at work. You can gather understanding from your coworkers, from the people you manage, and from the leaders of your organization to enlarge the way you see things and change the way you speak to and support the people around you—and even shift your own reasoning.

---

10 See also Mark Goulston and John Ullmen's article in *Harvard Business Review*, "How to Really Understand Someone Else's Point of View," April 22, 2013; blogs.hbr.org.

COLLABORATE WITH PEOPLE

- Spend a portion of your time listening to your peers.
- Adjust what you say.
- Acknowledge the other's intentions.
- Find out concerns of stakeholders and clients.
- Act like a pollinator with empathy you've developed.

LEAD A TEAM

- Pursue a regular schedule of formal listening sessions with each of your team members.
- Nurture creativity and help your team work well together.
- See how each person has changed so that you can measure the effectiveness of your cultivation.
- Shift how you support each person until it fits.

UNDERSTAND YOUR HIGHER-UPS

- Find out the reasoning and purpose behind each direction and request, so you can better support it.
- Search higher and higher up the hierarchy for a person who can explain these to you.
- Pushing back is not rebellion; it is collaboration—enabling a discussion to understand reasoning.

KNOW YOURSELF

- Understanding your reactions and triggers helps you focus and communicate better.
- Categorize what you say; is it reasoning, reaction, guiding principle, or is it opinion, conjecture, etc.?
- Recognize other people's emotions so you can check your own reaction and stay on track.
- Defer to your teammates when it's their turn.

Practical empathy helps you understand the purpose and methods of your organization.

CHAPTER 8

Apply Empathy Within Your Organization

Each organization exists for a purpose: to bring something to the world, make it available to people, and enable those people to capitalize upon it. Many organizations exist to also make a profit. Whether for profit or not, all organizations seek to sustain themselves, so they can continue bringing their things to the world. Within each organization, there is usually a healthy awareness of the purpose, as well as a focus on being sustainably successful.

> **NOTE** ORGANIZATIONS FOCUS ON BOTH SUCCESS AND SUPPORT
>
> **Success:** Enable the organization to continue achieving its purpose, which might be defined by profit, membership, giving, respect, invitations, or other metrics. An organization might change directions repeatedly in order to sustain itself.
>
> **Support:** Help people inside or outside the organization achieve their purposes; e.g., obtain what is needed, make better decisions, understand choices, enjoy something, feel safer, and so on.

Support and success are not opposites on a spectrum, but separate interests that are both important. Each waxes and wanes. When *success* and *support* are both robust, they can work hand-in-hand: support comes from good functionality and experiences for people and deep understanding for their aims. This strongly connected support, in turn, assures success.[1]

Even in small groups or teams, this success/support framework can be applied. For example, the board of a homeowner's association may contain only five people. *Success* means keeping the group active over the years, with interested members, and attracting new members when wanted. *Support* is providing collaboration, ideas, and a place for discussion where members and homeowners feel that they can contribute without censure. The opposite of this scenario is when a homeowner's association board fails to attract new members because the meetings are known for being forums for argument, aspersions, and judgments. Or where homeowners offering ideas at the meeting don't feel rewarded for exploring concepts. So even a small group like a board can benefit from wielding listening and empathy to support its members and sustain itself over time.

---

1 John Borthwick: "Venture capitalists judge a startup by whether it'll be a billion dollar company. They should judge by whether it can change the world," article by Erin Griffith on pandodaily.com, July 10, 2013.

See from Your Organization's Point of View

Sometimes it's really hard to tell whether your organization has a healthy level of interest in either success or support. Your organization's intentions might be muddled or not clearly communicated.

What you seek is larger than the motivations behind particular initiatives; it is the overall direction of the organization—its reason for being. Try to get a grasp on what you are doing as an organization and who you are doing it for, both externally and internally.

One way to clarify what the intentions are is to go back in history to the beginning of your organization. What was written then about the purpose being pursued? With long-lived organizations, this original purpose surely shifts. For example, in the United States, early airlines in the mid 1920s focused on getting airmail contracts from the U.S. Postal Service within local geographic regions, because the range a plane could fly was limited. To increase the throughput, nighttime operations were added. Soon after this change, these airlines started carrying a few passengers in addition to the mail. As plane technology improved, the decision-makers at the airlines aimed to fly longer distances, and eventually they established routes. These attracted more passengers than mail.

As airlines grew, their purpose shifted. Early purposes of the airlines were to get mail to its destination faster and to fly passengers to destinations safely. Lawmakers legislated fairness in mail contracts, safety, and access to airports. Later, the focus was on amenities and comfort, such as in-flight meals and better seating as the routes became longer. Then higher oil prices and labor costs started reversing the focus toward carrying the maximum number of passengers per flight. Several airlines focused on offering discounted, minimal services with shorter routes. Others focused on loyalty programs to retain customers. An industry downturn influenced by the hijackings and crashes of September 2001 caused the airlines to further minimize services, and they were also required to follow "security" processes to avert a repeat of the intentional crashes. Because of these conditions, many airlines in the U.S. merged. Now, one of the purposes of some airlines seems to be keeping passengers distracted while in flight, with amenities such as Wi-Fi, television, magazines, shopping, movies, and games, as well as communicating updates to passengers before flights.

Another way to understand your organization's purpose is to look at marketing taglines. Taglines do not necessarily represent the aim of the organization, but taglines are meant to communicate to an audience. Hence, they are a good place to see what decision-makers chose as a message to the people you support. They are also an indicator of whether the focus is on the offering itself or on the people being supported.

"Melts in your mouth, not in your hands" (M&M candy) and "All the news that's fit to print" (*New York Times*) both describe the offerings. "Just do it" (Nike); "Reach out and touch someone" (AT&T); "Thrive" (Kaiser Permanente); and "I've fallen, and I can't get up" (LifeCall) all imply a person's intent and related emotions.

An organization is only as strong as the humans within it. If all of you understand the purpose and direction of your organization clearly, imagine how powerful that would be. Every decision each one of you makes could be aimed at supporting the current purpose. There would be fewer complaints about work that seems pointless, and so on. While this vision is mostly fantasy, empathy for your organization can actually make a subtle difference.

If you can grasp the direction of the organization, then your own decisions and suggestions can aim in that direction.

Make Small Changes

When it comes to making suggestions to people internally, several barriers arise. What if changing something upsets the people who are happy with it now? Seth Godin, a well-known marketing expert, author, and speaker, says, "One of the most essential tasks a leader faces is understanding just how much the team is afraid of making things better."[2] So instead of emphasizing change, minimize it. Make small changes.

There are several things you can do that are small:

- Include support objectives in yearly goals.

- Seek the root cause of problems rather than fixing the structure or the approach.

---

2 See also Seth Godin's blog post "We Don't Need to Make It Better," February 5, 2013; sethgodin.typepad.com

- Pivot toward a slightly different direction based on the empathy you have developed.

- Don't let technology define your projects.

- Don't be too focused on methods or the need to hurry.

Include Support Objectives

With the empathy you developed, you are especially equipped to nudge the health of the *support* variable. For example, at an organizational level, maybe the last set of quarterly goals was worded with *success* objectives, and not with *support* objectives. You can collaborate with the people who wrote it to add *support* objectives, as well as key results to define how you hope to see *success* measured.[3]

You could apply a similar shift if your organization's tagline is unclear about support. This suggestion is not a small thing, however, and large organizations often hire agencies to develop their taglines. You might be able to volunteer yourself for the review committee.

Seek the Root Cause

When an organization seems to be faltering, one of the things decision-makers try to fix is how the company runs—the structure and the processes. They look at what exists presently and make changes in what are considered lever points. When this doesn't work, perhaps it's because the existing structure isn't the right fit in the first place. Try looking for the root problem. Empathy about the way your organization actually functions will help.

For example, if the root issue is that several departments want to "own the website," and the department that owns it now was recently invented, then it's probably a structure issue. In human history, there have been myriad solutions for how a group might achieve objectives. There have been many structures for governing, for trade, for battle, and for building. Some of these structures have even been inspired by the natural world. For example, a hive of bees contains a single entity directing all activity, the queen. A corporate hierarchy is *somewhat* derived from this natural structure, with the

---

3 See more about the OKR (Objectives and Key Results) approach from Christina Wodtke in her Interaction14 conference presentation and blog post. www.eleganthack.com, "The Executioner's Tale" and "The Art of the OKR," February 1, 2014.

idea that control is hierarchical. Is there another structure out there or in history that could inspire a way of working together that takes into account human tendencies? Are there other approaches used in less-known contexts from which you can derive a process of working together? Thought experiments like these might lead to discussion, which might lead to a small change.

Pivot

In new organizations and start-ups, there is great pressure to be successful quickly. Small groups scramble to test out their idea under real conditions, and when things don't look encouraging, they shift their course a bit. This is call a *pivot*, which means taking a step in a slightly different direction while using the knowledge you've gathered to support the decision. A great foundation for this knowledge includes the empathy you've developed with those you intend to support, your understanding of those who are guiding or funding your effort, and empathy about how your group collaborates best.

Don't Let Technology Define Your Projects

With every fresh wave of hardware and software, there comes excitement about harnessing it for your organization's advantage. Decision-makers discuss the advantages of making solutions for this platform or that environment. They might focus, for example, on the ability of a mobile device to be location aware or what a movement sensor can sense. This means they are, regrettably, building solutions for the GPS and for the accelerometer. That's how it gets phrased, too. "We're building an app for the iPhone that takes advantage of location-awareness." People don't seem to come into the equation until after it's produced.

When you hear these phrases in discussion, use your empathetic mindset to ask about the purpose behind it. Bring up the subject of the people whom it will serve. Repeat some of the things you heard while developing empathy. The excitement of something new that couldn't be done before is good for the energy of a team, so try not to deflate it. Simply sharpen it and redirect it, toward a stronger purpose in support of people.[4]

---

4 See also James Kalbach's matrix of technology innovation in his blog post "Clarifying Innovation: Four Zones of Innovation," experiencinginformation. wordpress.com, June 3, 2012, and Des Traynor's post on the Intercom.io blog, "How to Predict Technology Flops," October 13, 2014.

Many organizations still define new initiatives by the way a
person might access it. "That's the mobile app project." "That's
the kiosk initiative." "This is the project we're doing for subscrip-
tions." Gently try to guide this tendency toward project names
that reference the people you are trying to support. Next time
you say, "We are building X for Y," make absolutely sure the Y is
the name of the types of humans you are trying to support.

Don't Be Too Focused on Methods and Speed

Adding to the ways an organization can get snared by its own habits
are methodologies. It's easy to get caught up in the day-to-day steps
of a technique and cease to think about how applicable the results
are, or how you might use a different approach for a new scenario.
If you are good at using a hammer, then lots of things look like nails.
Many groups do have a way of staying up-to-date with evolving
methodologies, and can thereby audit the effectiveness of what they
are doing. You can help your team by periodically asking yourself,
"Are we doing this because it's what we do?"

A specific example of one of these habits is how organizations foster
a sense of hurry. There are many reasons to hurry: be first to market
with a new idea, keep up with the competition, finish before spending deadlines, make the most of limited funding, adhere to a strict
production schedule or a seasonal horizon, etc. While every culture
seems to have a saying about how hurrying makes for poor-quality
craftsmanship, these maxims are often ignored by most business processes. You can't slow down the processes at your organization, but
you can introduce a slow-rhythm process. Continuously collecting
stories, developing empathy with the people your organization supports, dipping into this process every couple of months—this is the
unhurried approach that yields fine workmanship. Add this routine
of collecting knowledge at a slow frequency in parallel with all the
other work going on at your organization.

Blaze a Trail from Established Paths

Without consciously realizing it, you and the decision-makers at your organization might be contributing to a mindless chase. The quarry might be new technology, or the quarry might be the competition. You might get swept up in the excitement to be first to market with a new technology, first to invent or discover something, or first to leverage new functionality. The big idea captures all your attention. On the other hand, copying what has been successful for other organizations in their market feels risk-free. You might be so focused on technology and the competition that you forget to measure the worth of an idea against a particular audience's purpose. The overall focus of your organization is on racing to get ahead of the other organizations, rather than an effort to truly be supportive of people.

Of course, there are organizations, or branches of organizations, whose sole purpose is to constantly push the boundaries of what is technically feasible. These are usually research groups. In these cases, the people they aim to support are those professionals who might, in turn, make use of the discoveries in support of people who can benefit from it. Research groups can be exempt from focusing on end-customers, but in many cases, such as pharmaceutical research, a detailed understanding of humans helps researchers choose the promising paths.

The fear of being left behind represents a real risk. What if your organization doesn't offer as broad a set of services as the other company? Won't people flock to the other offering and leave you? This is a zero-sum mindset, where features or services make up the numbers in the calculation. And it's quite a compelling argument. Supporting people is not a zero-sum game. However, innovation and creativity are not zero-sum either because new ideas keep getting added to the equation, continually unbalancing it.

There is a middle road. That road combines all the tactics: innovate because it's possible, keep up with the competition, and manage risk. The key is to add your knowledge of real people and differing purposes to your focus on what's possible and what the competition is doing.

Think of it like blazing a trail through the mountains. All the competitors are toiling along the same valley, jostling to be in the first position. The trail gets defined by different leaders in this competitive rotation, which means there is no individual strategic direction. Because you have worked to understand the larger intentions of the people you support, you have effectively been exploring nearby terrain. You can confidently branch off the well-trodden trail and form new tracks and loops outside of that particular valley (see Figure 8.1). The empathetic mindset helps your organization map out more of this unknown territory, so you can confidently branch away from competitors.

FIGURE 8.1

This photo depicts the mountainous region around Tuolumne, California, during winter. If you know the terrain, you can confidently go off-trail. The same goes for knowing the people you support—you can confidently depart from what the competition is pursuing.

Address the Broader Landscape

There is often a sense that you can grab your piece of land by marking it out with a unique idea. In particular, this is a widespread undercurrent of the digital arena. Consequently, services and apps get launched that address the generalization of a problem. They make no attempt to address subtleties or perspectives that might represent different audiences. And while it used to be true that you could launch a simple version of a digital service or product and people would flock to it, it's not a frontier anymore. There are many neighbors in the community now.

Typical digital services and apps are not complex or interconnected. When a frontier changes into a settled landscape, among the changes are the way that participants specialize. The general store gets replaced with a hardware store, a dry goods store, and a pharmacy, etc. A baker comes to town, and years later there are bakers from five different cultures, each offering their traditional breads and pastries—each supporting the nostalgia or the adventurousness of different people. The bakers source their ingredients from different specialists, and depend upon different craftspeople to update and maintain their different types of ovens. Not only is there variety, but also each specialist continually strives to make the best connections with peers, service providers, and customers. A larger community develops.

The empathetic mindset helps you learn how to specialize and how to form a network. Aim to build for the long term, with the idea that you fill a niche in a complex ecosystem of services.

Practice These Skills

Even if there's not a chance in the world that you can change the way your organization works, you can still benefit personally from trying out these concepts. If you can clarify for yourself what drives your organization as a whole, the knowledge can't help but influence the way you do your work. If you discuss these drivers with people you work with, together your small component of the organization might make decisions that more effectively support people.

Practice: Clarify the Purpose

The purpose of your organization may or may not be clear. Either way, this exercise will edify you and your immediate peers.

1. Examine the history of your organization. Chart the path it has followed through the years. Try to summarize the purpose the organization had during different eras, if it has been around for a long time.

2. Look at the tagline and various marketing campaigns the organization has sponsored over the past several years. If you can, ask people who were responsible for the campaigns what the decision-making process was and what philosophies the ads represent. Summarize these meanings.

3. Write the clearest summary you can of the current purpose of the organization.

4. In all your notations, notice when the purpose has had a healthy focus on both success and support, and when it has leaned more in one direction than the other. Also check whether technology or methodology seemed to drive the decisions. Finally, note how audiences were defined, whether by needs or behavior or not at all. These will all fluctuate over time, but it's good to see what has happened.

Summary

It's not common to focus on your organization's purpose in the world. When you make an effort to understand how the organization measures its success and defines its support for people, it will help you with your own decisions. Knowing the landscape in which your organization operates will allow you to branch out confidently to new terrain.

SEE FROM YOUR ORGANIZATION'S POINT OF VIEW

- How has the organization's purpose changed since its beginning?
- Do the taglines describe the offering or refer to the intent of the people it supports?

MAKE SMALL CHANGES

- Include support objectives in your yearly goals.
- Seek the root cause of problems and try to fix that rather than the structure or approach.
- Pivot toward a slightly different direction based on the empathy you have developed.
- Don't let technology define your projects.
- Establish a slow pulse of continuous empathy development.

BLAZE A TRAIL FROM ESTABLISHED PATHS

- What is the organization's goal? Innovation for its own sake? Keeping up with the competition? Other?
- Confidently branch off the well-trodden path based on the knowledge you've gathered about people you support.

ADDRESS THE BROADER LANDSCAPE

- The empathetic mindset helps you specialize.
- Build for interconnections with other players in the community.
- Build for sustainability and longevity.

Zero in on where you can mix
practical empathy into
your own work.

CHAPTER 9

Where Do You Go from Here?

As a good professional, you know to balance your own reasoning and guiding principles with those of your customers, your team, and your organization. However, perfect balance is not feasible all the time. Practicing the empathetic mindset as the years go by will help with your balance. More than any other thing, practice will steadily bring you confidence and experience.

If practice is the key, then demonstrating the empathetic mindset to those you work with is the treasure room. Being the person who plays the role without preaching or persuading is the most effective way of spreading the idea. Here are just a couple of ideas to help you bring the empathetic mindset into your own organization.

Explain It to Others

You can explain the empathetic mindset without persuading. You can even explain it without using words like "empathy," just in case there's a chance that those words will turn off your listener.

The empathetic mindset gives you powerful vision. Like a pair of glasses that you put on and take off, you dip into this mindset in order to focus on things—people, specifically. As you uncover their deeper thinking, you add to the reservoir of what you know about reasoning, reactions, and guiding principles that drive different people. This reservoir is not full of answers to your problems, but instead it is full of catalysts to your thinking. It's like putting yourself in a relaxed frame of mind to allow for that stroke of creativity or insight.

These empathetic reservoirs are not necessarily going to influence the outcome of your decision or the design of a thing you are creating. Instead, the inspiration from these reservoirs guides the direction of your decisions, the flow of a design, and the conceptual basis for an idea. The empathetic mindset is the background and foundation that your professional thinking relies on.

When you explain this to someone else, you may also want to mention that the empathetic mindset is known as *cognitive empathy* and that *emotional empathy* is different. Emotional empathy is when someone's emotion causes you similar feelings and memories. The best practical use of emotional empathy is to notice when it has happened and use that awareness to return your curiosity to what underlies the other person's behavior. This curiosity is difficult to maintain if you're distracted by your own emotions and memories.

Additionally, you may want to explain that developing and applying empathy exclusively focuses on people and completely avoids contemplation of solutions. Checking how well a solution might work for a person is a different exercise, one that falls under the category of evaluation. Developing empathy is for the express purpose of generating inspiration.

Go Small

The best thing you can do for yourself is to build your confidence. Confidence doesn't result if you set big expectations and then have to struggle to achieve them. The aim is that you don't get to the end of a cycle of listening to people and feel relieved that it's over. Instead, the aim is that it didn't take all your energy. Keep it to small sets of two or five or 10 people and keep repeating it every couple of months. Small sets ensure that you won't dread doing the next set.

An ongoing cycle will let you build a repository of knowledge. Each cycle can be tailored to upcoming efforts, exploring challenges that you expect to face in the near future. If "the near future" is actually closer than a couple of weeks, even just one listening session will help.

If You Do Only One Thing

Mix it up.

Do everything in moderation—and this applies to how you wield the empathetic mindset. You are not expected to embrace everything written here wholesale. Instead, incorporate bits and pieces into your regular work practice. Adapt the ideas that you like and bend them to fit in with other philosophies and approaches you follow. Of course, "everything in moderation" is a guiding principle, which you might not follow. If that's the case, then go ahead and adopt all of this.

Nothing in this book is meant as canon. None of it is meant to argue that other approaches are not as valid; they are each valid and effective in their own way. Mix them together.

Secret Agenda

Throughout this book, there has been a theme of humility. Self-restraint is key to being able to open up to other people's thoughts and ideas. But you don't have to bury your ego entirely—only when you are in the empathetic mindset. It's not a spiritual practice, but a practical way to broaden your understanding of the people you hope to support. The goal is to make whatever you're doing work out better for other people. These other people—and the people you collaborate with—will help you explore different paths. The decisions you make as a result of these explorations can be influenced by your own experience and ego, and by the circumstances around you.

As populations around the globe increase and communication technology shrinks distances between everybody, you will find yourself working with a wider and wider variety of people. To collaborate smoothly and to really make a difference for the people you support, the empathetic mindset will help you ensure each other's success.

INDEX

personal contribution, and lack of
listening, 8–9
personal distress, 24
personas, 117–118
person-focused research, 37
persuasion
empathy used for, 38
explaining empathetic mindset
without, 172
phrases, 106
pivot, 162
practice
applying empathy within
organizations, 167
empathetic mindset, 26–27
empathy with coworkers, 153–154
idea-generation, 133–134
self-awareness, 150–152
preferences, as representation of deeper
reasoning, 89
process explanations, studying what
was said, 86
product strategy, 4
purchasing-behavior segments, 118–119

Q

qualitative data analysis, 5
quantitative data analysis, 3, 5
quote-collection exercise, 82–83

R

reactions
emotional, 55
listening for, 55
neutralizing during listening session,
69–72
and self-awareness, 152
reading written summaries out
loud, 102
reasoning
deductive, 114
developing empathy, 39
listening for, 54
rebalancing the organization, 14
recording formal listening sessions, 41
religion, emotional literacy in, 71
remote listening, 43–44
report-writing, 141

research groups, 164
respect, showing in listening session,
67–69
root cause, applying empathy within
organizations, 161–162

S

scenarios, in idea-generation session, 121
scene explanations, studying what was
said, 86
scientific terminology, abuse of, 6
scope, studying what was said, 91
self empathy, 25
self-awareness, 148–152
self-focused progress, 8
self-restraint and humility, 174
sentence-diagramming, 98–99
solution-focused research, 37
spiritual quotes, 71
stages of developing and applying
empathy, 35–39
statement of fact, studying what was
said, 86
static documentation, 125
story of why, 3–5
studying what was said
concepts out of scope, 91
conjecture, 90–91
generalizations, 90
as listening practice, 91
making sense of concepts, 84–85
opinions, 87–89
passive behavior, 90
picking out concepts each participant
describes, 81–85
preferences, 89
process, scene, and event
explanations, 86
quote-collection exercise, 82–83
spending time with other person's
thoughts, 80
statements of facts, 86
what not to skip, 85–91
written summaries, 81
clarification, 98
compound sentences, avoiding,
100–101
conveying emotional reactions as
verbs, 95–97

ACKNOWLEDGMENTS

I am grateful to the people who offered enthusiasm, critique, and support. Thank you.

For sticking with me through the journey of making this book happen: Lou Rosenfeld

For his charming illustrations, which express the concepts in ways that words would fail: Brad Colbow

For background discussions, references, and pointers: Shujie Zhu, Stephanie Noble, Karl Fast, Mike Oren, Daniel Szuc, Peter Morville, Brian Winters, Lisa Lurie, Julie Ratner, Karen Lindemann, Murray Grigo-McMahon, Kristian Simsarian, Troy Effner

For conceptual critique, over food and/or chocolate: Christina Wodtke, Rainey Straus, Poornima Vijayashanker, Harry Max, Ted Weinstein, David Kadavy

For inspiring tweets, articles, and presentations: Erika Hall, Kim Goodwin, Leah Buley, Kelly Goto, Karen McGrane, Irene Au, Nilofer Merchant, Nate Bolt, Dave Gray, Dan Brown, Marcin Treder, Mark Weiser, Patrick Whitney, Dana Chisnell, Brene Brown, Cheryl Strayed, Rebecca Mauleon, Pema Chodron, Alain de Botton, Seth Godin, David Kelley, Tom Kelley, James Thurber, Dan Klyn, Daniel Goleman

For the review and critique of drafts: Carolyn Wan, Mike Oren, Susan Weinschenk, Peter Morville, Daniel Szuc, Jonathan Baker, Alisan Atvur, Lou Rosenfeld

For suggesting good FAQs: Stefan Freimark, Andrew Fung

For helping me out of linguistic conundrums and mild aphasia: Grammar Girl, Thesaurus.com, Philip Ramsey, Marta Justak

For reminding me to write in a translatable way: Stanley Chung, Masaki Sawamura, Wen Kai Qi, Jikun Liu

For keeping me healthy: Lucy Simon, Marjorie Forman, Gus Young

ABOUT THE AUTHOR

Indi Young is an independent consultant. She helps teams with person-focused research, design strategy, interaction flow, communications, and information architecture. She has been a trail-blazer of experience design since the dot-com boom, using her roots in computer science to help people adopt a neutral, well-considered mindset. In 2001, she was a founder of Adaptive Path, the San Francisco experience design agency. In 2008, her book, *Mental Models: Aligning Design Strategy with Human Behavior,* was published. She writes articles, conducts workshops and webinars, and speaks about the importance of pushing the boundaries of your perspective. You can follow her on Twitter @indiyoung or at www.indiyoung.com.